D0717750

Written by Moira Butterfield
Scoubidou models by Angela Bernardi

Edited by Philippa Wingate
Designed by Zoe Quayle
Assistant designer: Angela Bernardi
Illustrations by Garry Walton
Photography by Zul Mukhida
Additional illustrations by Paul Middlewick
Production by Joanne Rooke

Super-Stylin' Scoubidou

Annual 2006

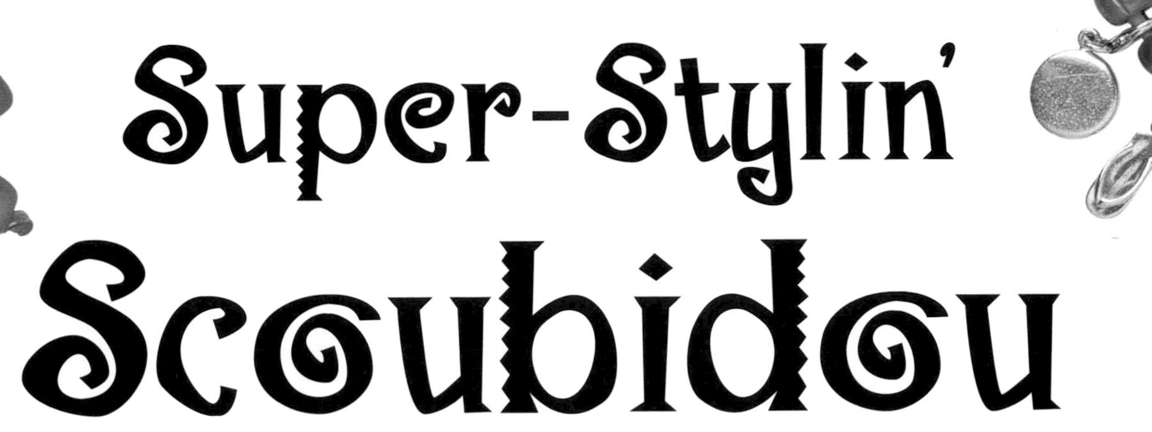

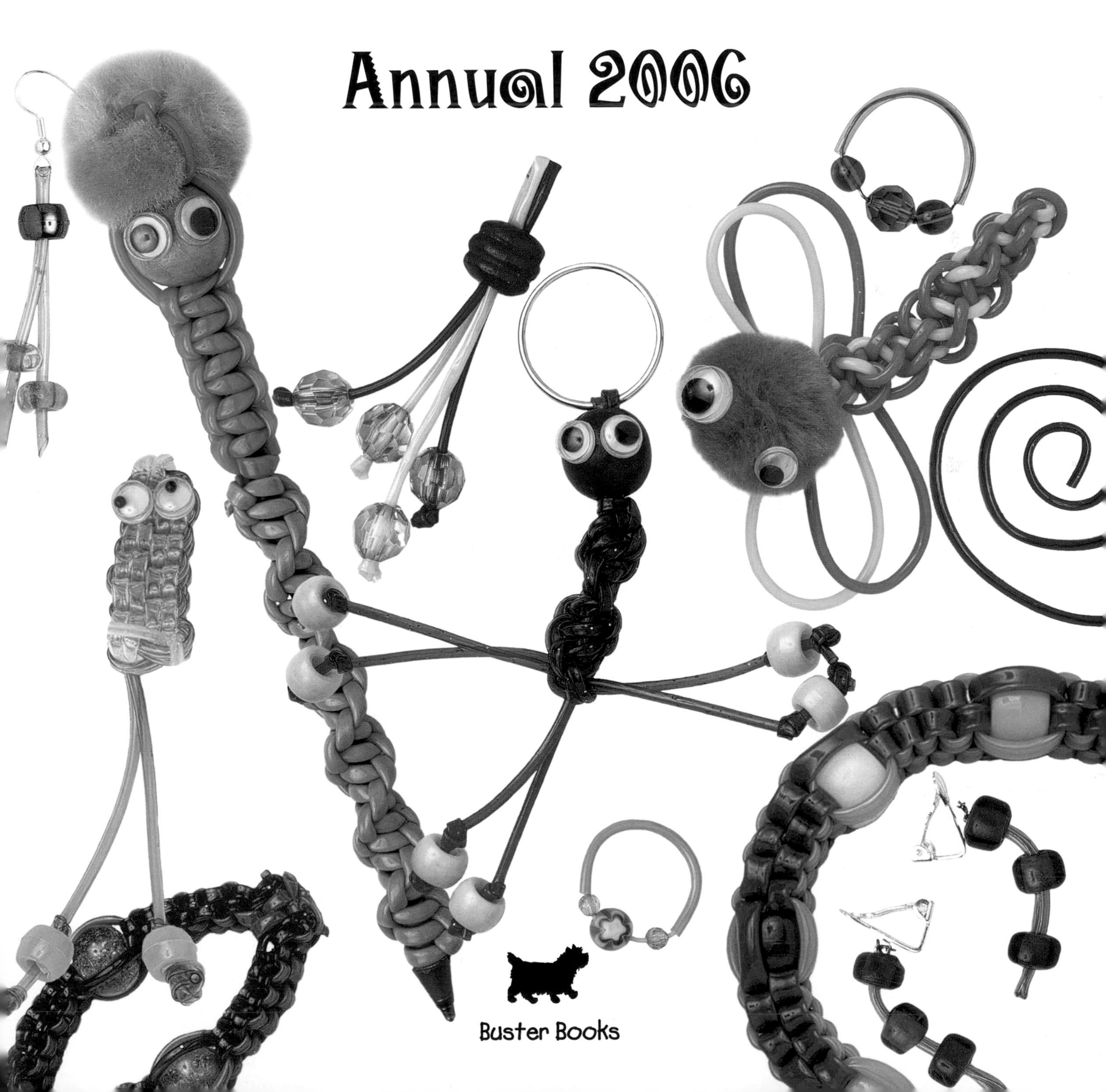

Buster Books

First published in Great Britain in 2005 by Buster Books,
an imprint of Michael O'Mara Books Limited,
9 Lion Yard, Tremadoc Road,
London SW4 7NQ
www.mombooks.com/busterbooks

Copyright © 2005 Buster Books

All rights reserved.
No part of this book may be reproduced, stored in a retrieval system, or transmitted in any form or by any means, electronic, mechanical, photocopying, recording or otherwise without the prior written permission of the copyright owners.

A CIP catalogue record for this book is available from the British Library.

ISBN 1-905158-18-1

2 4 6 8 10 9 7 5 3 1

Printed and bound in Italy by L.E.G.O.

Contents

Scoubidous Rock!

Everybody's doing it – movie stars on the sets of their films, models while they wait for their photo shoots, girls preparing totally hot looks for a night out.
What are we talking about? Scoubidous of course!
You can plait them, knot them, bead them and twist them, to create deeply divine and totally funky looks. No wonder the world's gone scoubidou crazy!
But exactly what is a scoubidou . . . ?

If non-scoubidou-ers want to know what a scoubidou is, tell them a scoubidou or a scoubie is a long length of plastic, like spaghetti, but hollow in the middle, like a tube.

Tell them scoubidous are really cheap (and casually mention that your birthday's coming up).

Tell them scoubidous come in loads of bright colours, including glitter, neon and glow-in-the-dark.

Tell them that anyone with a passion for fashion can make awesome things from scoubidous, including seriously hip jewellery, keyrings, and funny critters.

A scoubidou fact file

- Scoubidous usually come in 100cm lengths.
- Some scoubies are made of clear plastic. They look great mixed with coloured ones, because the colour shines through them.
- Scoubies come in different thicknesses. You should always use scoubies that are the same thickness, otherwise your scoubies could end up looking lumpy.
- You can buy scoubies in your local toy store or order them over the Internet (see page 55).

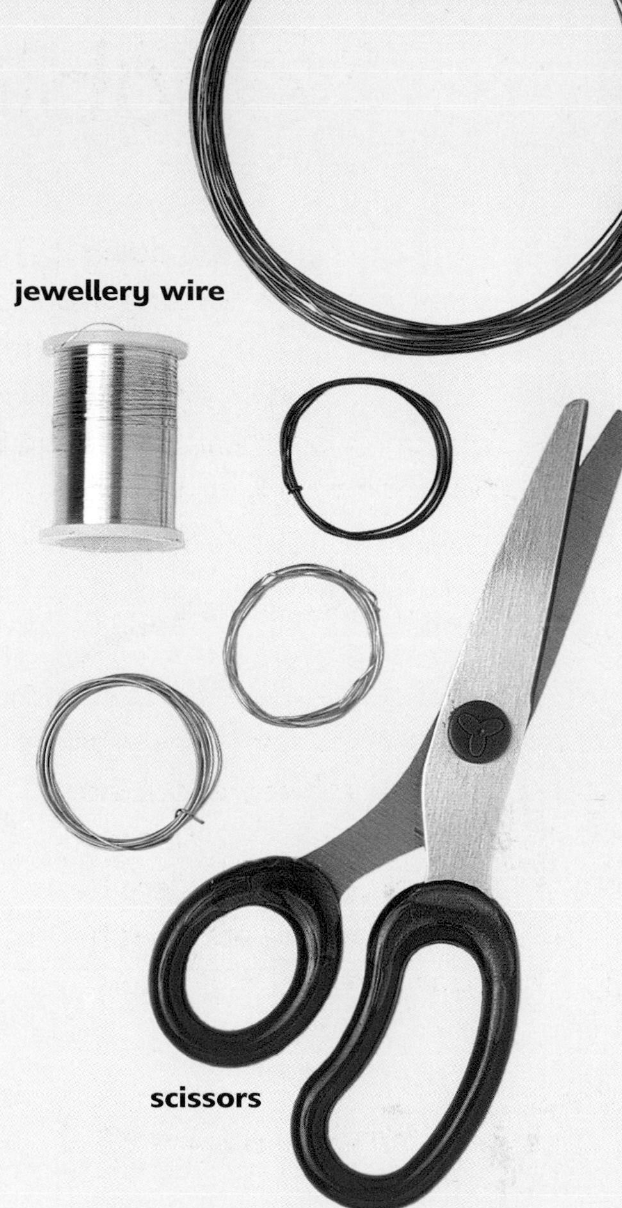

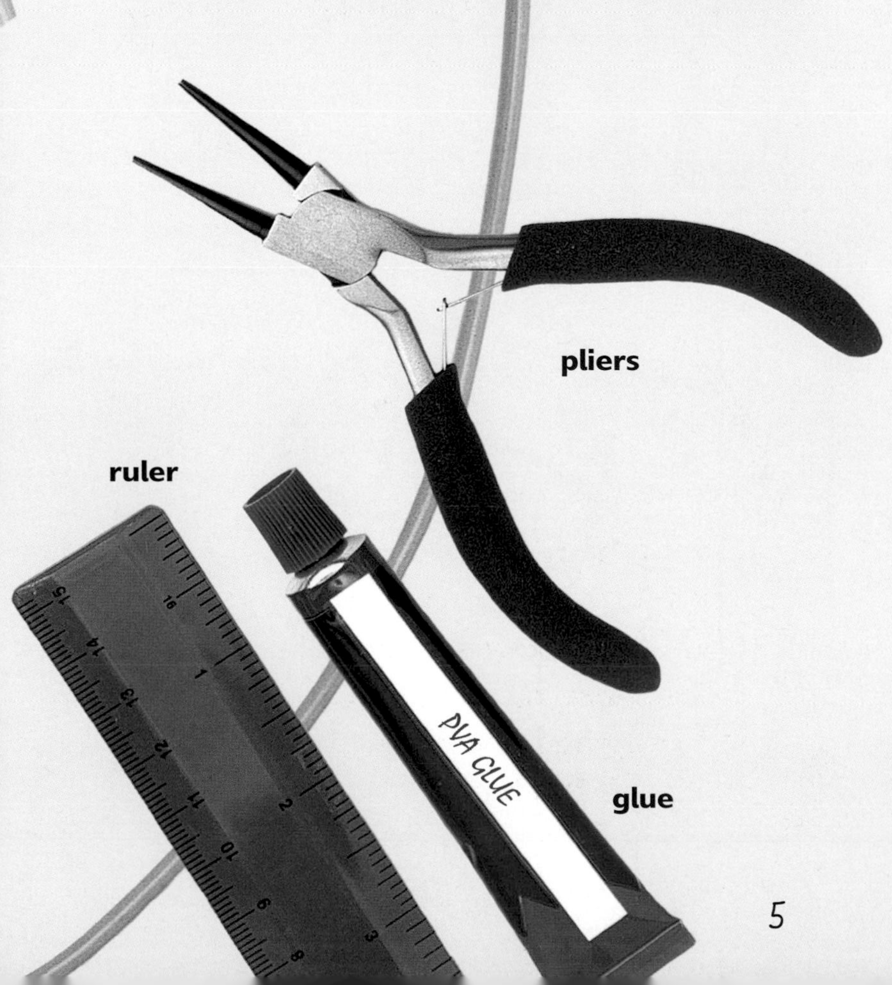

Scoubidou essentials

At the beginning of each project in this book you will find a list of what you need. In addition to the things listed, you will need a pair of scissors, a pair of pliers, some PVA glue, a ruler and some fine jewellery wire.

You'll see a selection of all the other extras you might want to use on page 56. You can buy these from craft shops or scoubidou Internet sites (see page 55).

Let's Get Started

Once upon a time there was a crazy genius who guarded the secret 'starter knot', the key to scoubidous. Well, OK . . . that's not true . . . but the starter knot is important because it's the first stitch you do on most scoubidou projects.

Practise it a few times and soon you'll be ready to create your own slammin' scoubies.

You will need:

- Two scoubidous the same length, but different colours
- Awesome patience when you first get started!

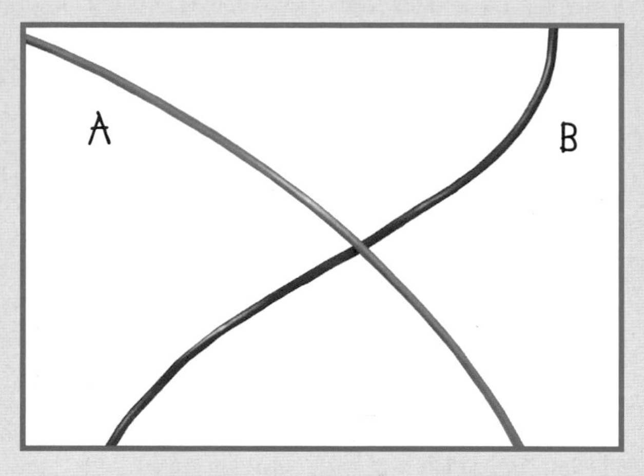

1. Lay strand A across the middle of strand B, in a cross shape.

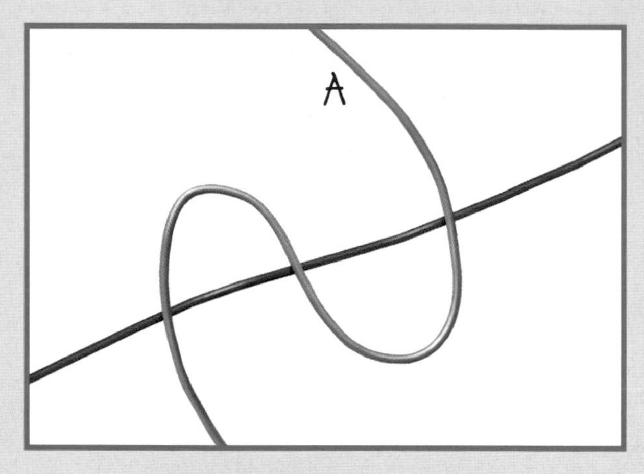

2. Use strand A to make a loop going upwards and a loop going downwards.

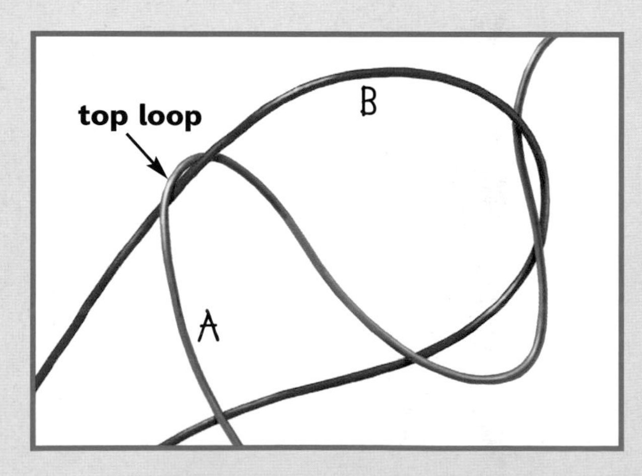

3. Thread the right-hand end of B through A's top loop.

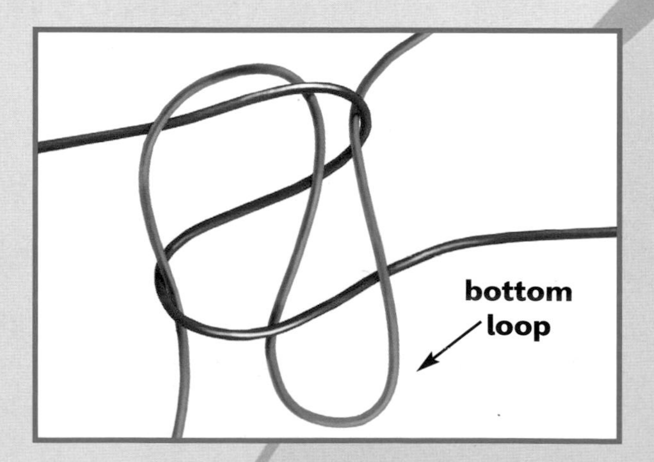

4. Thread the left-hand end of B through A's bottom loop.

5. Pull the four strands carefully to make a knot that looks like a little cushion.

A starter knot looks like this. Magic, huh?

Ask your mates

When you first start using scoubidous, ask any of your friends who already know how to help you crack the secret of scoubies.

Square That Scoubie

Here comes scoubie secret number two – the square stitch. You can use it to make cool keyrings, sassy bracelets and loads of other funky scoubie stuff.

Follow these step-by-step instructions carefully to square that scoubie and make a really cool keyring.

You will need:

- Two scoubidous the same length, but different colours (different colours make the stitch easier to understand)
- A split ring (see page 56)

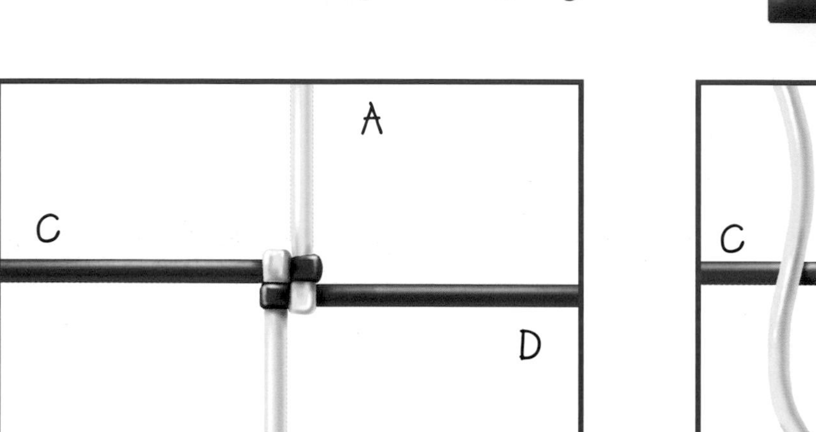

1. Begin by making a starter knot (see page 6). Hold it between your thumb and forefinger.

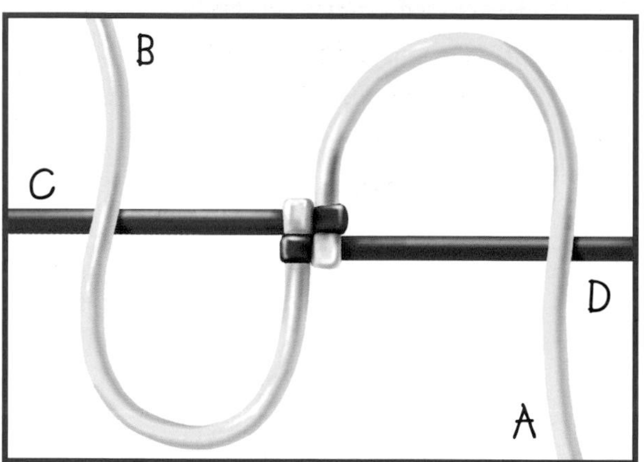

2. Now make a top loop and a bottom loop, exactly as shown above.

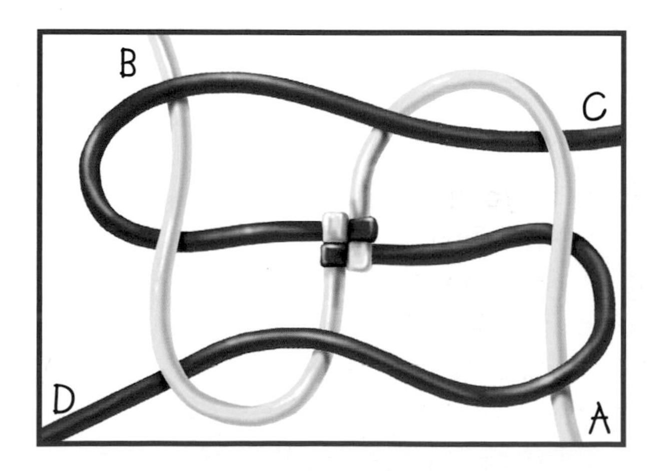

3. First thread strand C over B and through loop A. Then thread strand D over A and through loop B. Pull all four strands tight.

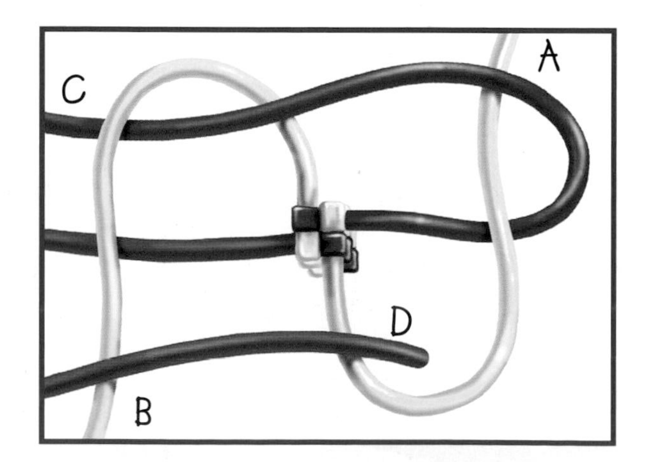

4. Now make a top loop and a bottom loop as shown above. First thread C as shown. Then thread D as shown. Pull tight.

5. Keep working between steps **2** and **4** to get a row of square stitches. Pull the last stitch tight (find out how to finish off your scoubidou row on page 11).

6. Push a split ring gently through your starter knot. If you like, knot pretty beads on the loose ends.

To add a bead, place it on top of your last stitch, and make two more stitches on top of the bead to hold it in place.

If you leave your finished scoubidou overnight it will 'set', which means the knots and stitches will stay more firmly in place.

Circle Scoubie Session

Here is scoubie secret number three – the circle stitch. It makes a different-shaped scoubie row to the square stitch, and you can use it in any project you want.

It only takes two scoubies to start going in circles!

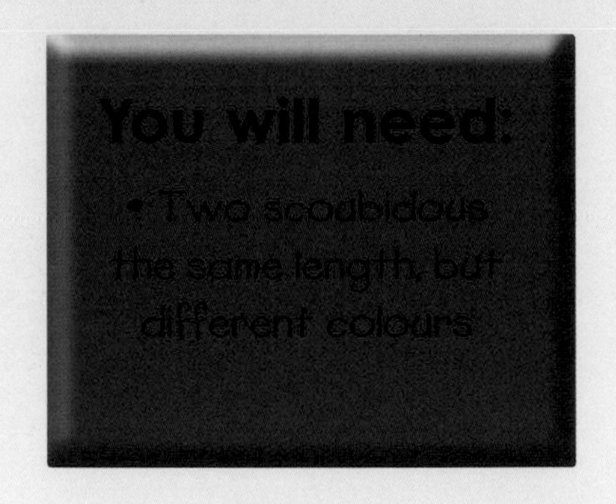

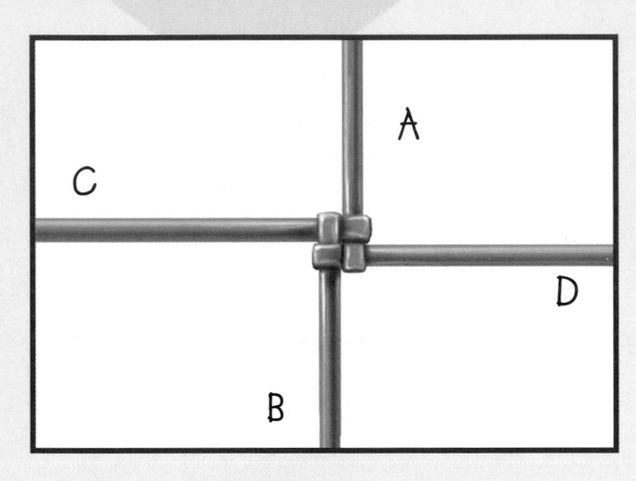

1. Begin by making a starter knot (see page 6). Hold it between your thumb and forefinger.

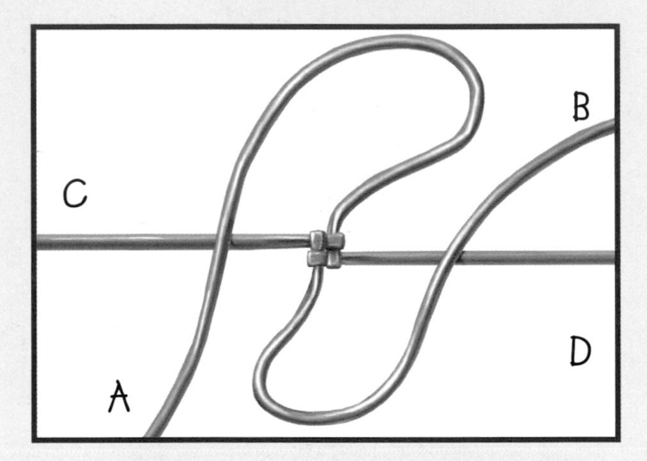

2. Make a loop on the top with end A and a loop on the bottom with end B, as shown above.

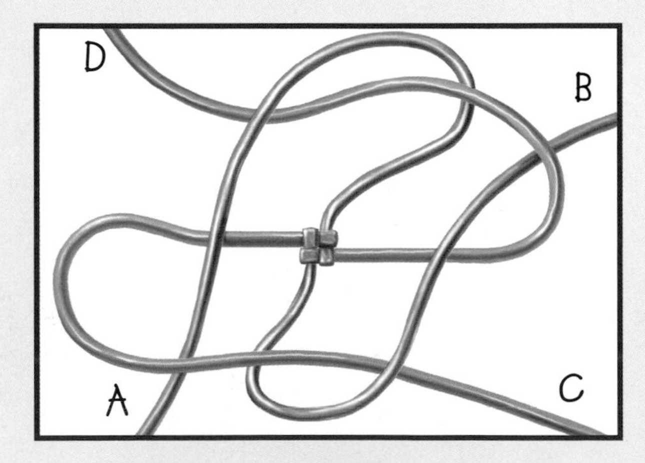

3. Thread end D over B and through the top loop. Thread end C over A through the bottom loop.

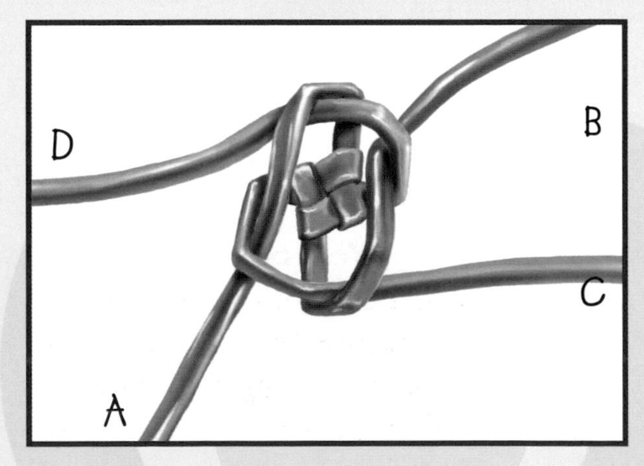

4. Tighten the knot. Repeat steps **2** and **3** again and again, to get a row of round scoubie stitches.

How can I extend my scoubie row?

It's easy to add a new scoubie strand to a row of circle or square stitch. Take a new strand and fold it in half to find the middle. Lay the middle of the strand on top of your last stitch. Hold the new strand in place and make two stitches with the old strands over the top of the new one. Pull the stitches tight before you trim the loose ends off. Now carry on stitching with the new scoubie.

A row of round stitches looks totally funkalicious.

How do I finish off my scoubie row?

The easiest way to finish off a row of scoubie stitching is to pull the last stitch really tight. Add a dab of glue to it and then trim off the loose ends.

Another method is to take two strands which are diagonally opposite each other and tie them in a simple knot. Then trim the loose ends. Take the remaining two strands and do the same.

Hip Zip Tassels

Fancy a career in fashion design? Start with some scoubidou zip tassels to fit on to the zip of your favourite coats, tops and bags. They couldn't be simpler to make and are the perfect way to glam up any outfit, bag or accessory.

Be warned, once everyone sees how groovalicious the tassels are, they'll all want one.

You will need:

- Two scoubidous
- A split ring
- Small beads
- Some bigger, fatter beads

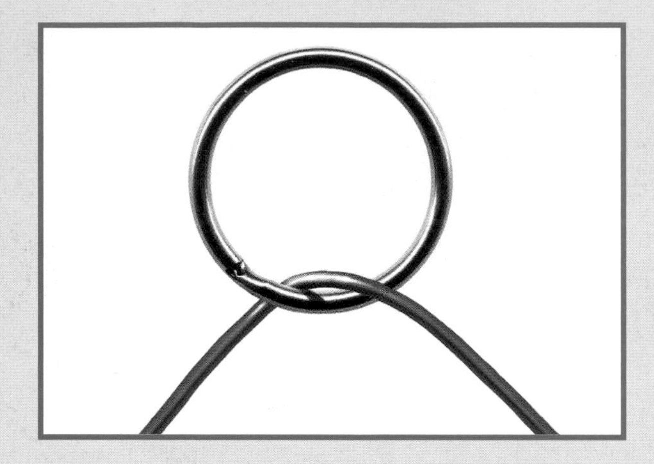

1. Thread one scoubidou half way through the split ring.

2. Tightly knot the other scoubidou round the first one, up against the split ring.

either

Tie a knot in each scoubie strand. Then thread on a bead, and tie another knot beneath it.

or

Push a fat bead up to the top of the scoubies. Knot them together beneath it.

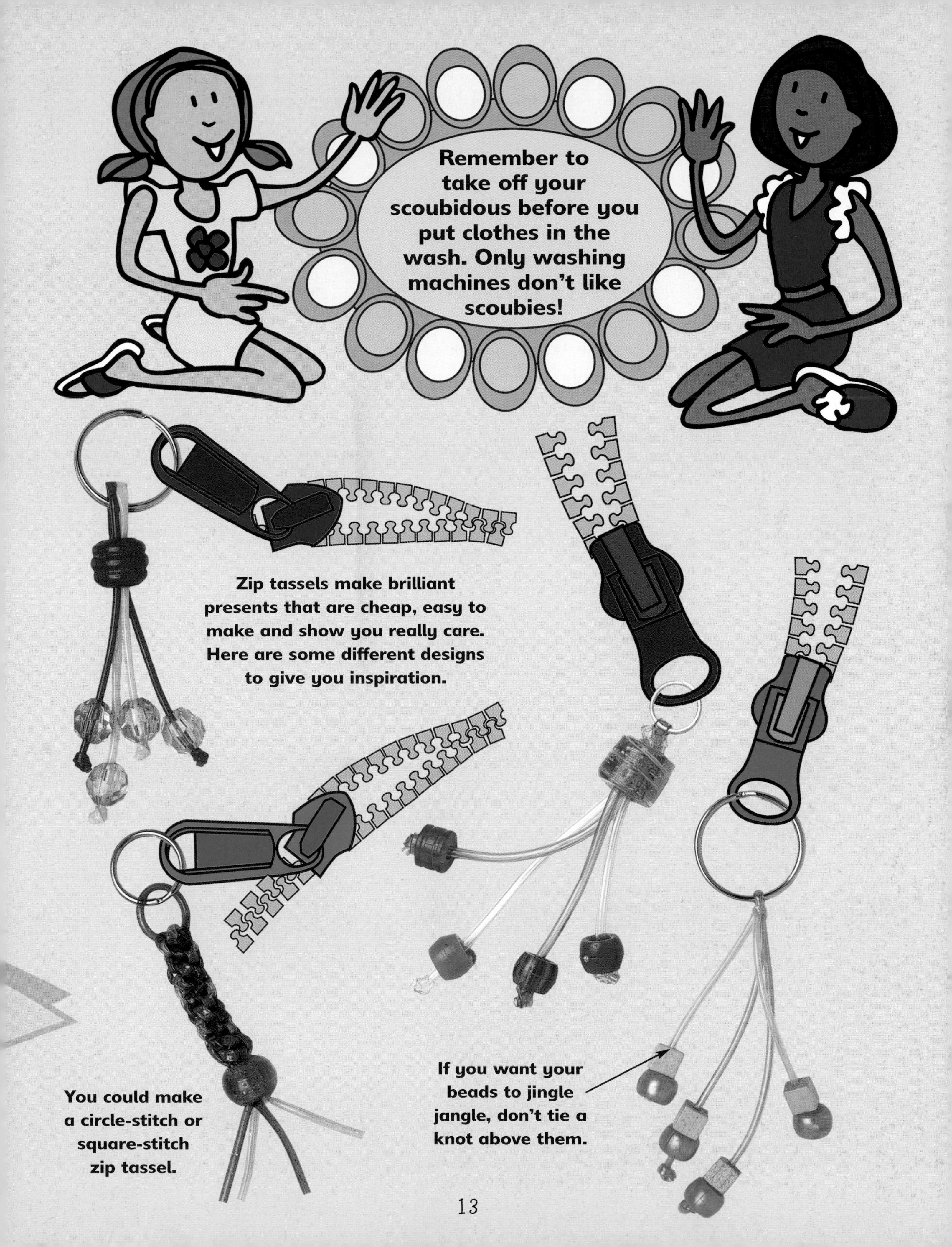

Zip tassels make brilliant presents that are cheap, easy to make and show you really care. Here are some different designs to give you inspiration.

You could make a circle-stitch or square-stitch zip tassel.

If you want your beads to jingle jangle, don't tie a knot above them.

Scoubie Staircase

Here is scoubie secret number four – the scoubie staircase stitch. It's called the staircase stitch because it looks like a spiral staircase – simple! Whatever you decide to call it, you'll find it's a super-quick way to make any scoubie project. When you have made a row of spiral stitches you can make it into a cool bracelet.

You will need:

- Two scoubidous the same length, but different colours

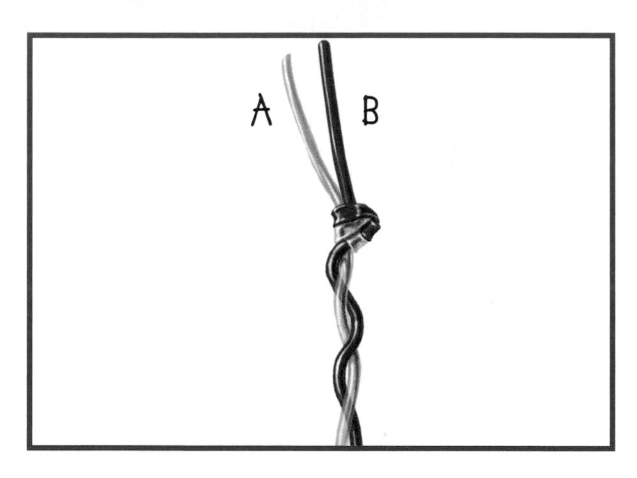

1. Tie the scoubies together. Wrap scoubie A around scoubie B for about 2cm.

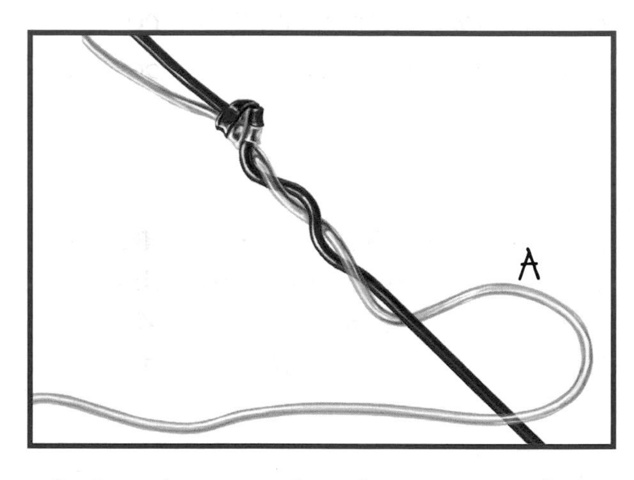

2. Now lay scoubie A over scoubie B, from right to left, making a loop.

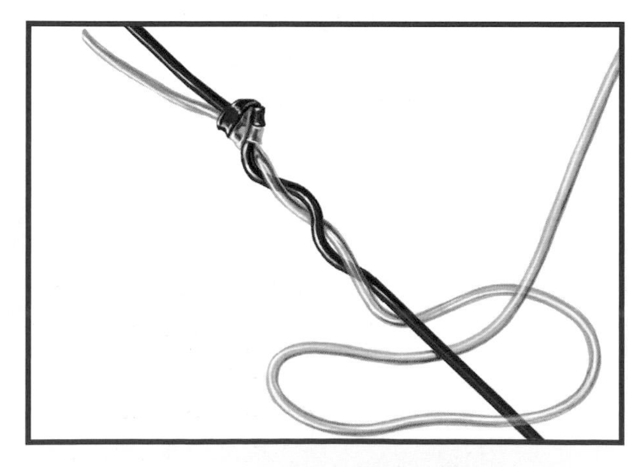

3. Thread scoubie A around, behind scoubie B, and then back through the loop. Pull it tight to make a knot.

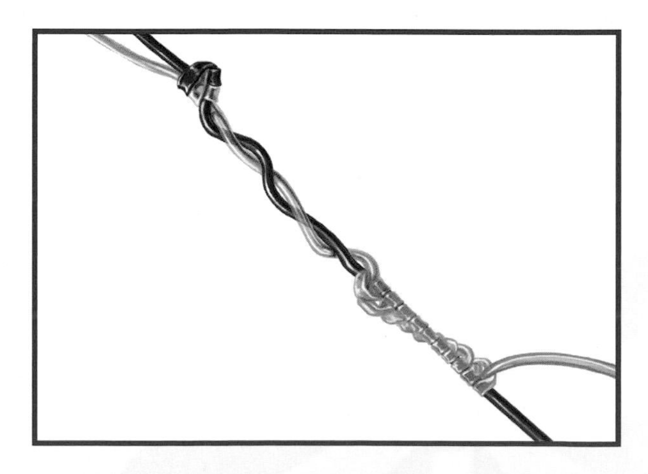

4. Keep repeating steps **2** and **3**, pulling the knots evenly together as you go. Hey presto! Your scoubie staircase will begin to appear.

How can I lengthen a scoubie staircase?

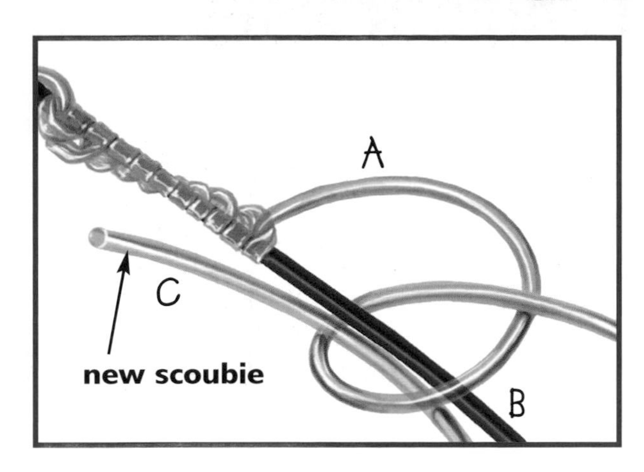

1. Lay scoubie C, the new scoubie, alongside scoubie B. Carry on stitching with A, locking in scoubie C.

2. Start knotting with scoubie C. Cut the loose ends of A and C close to the bracelet, so they do not stick out. Finish with a row of twisting and a knot, as per step 1.

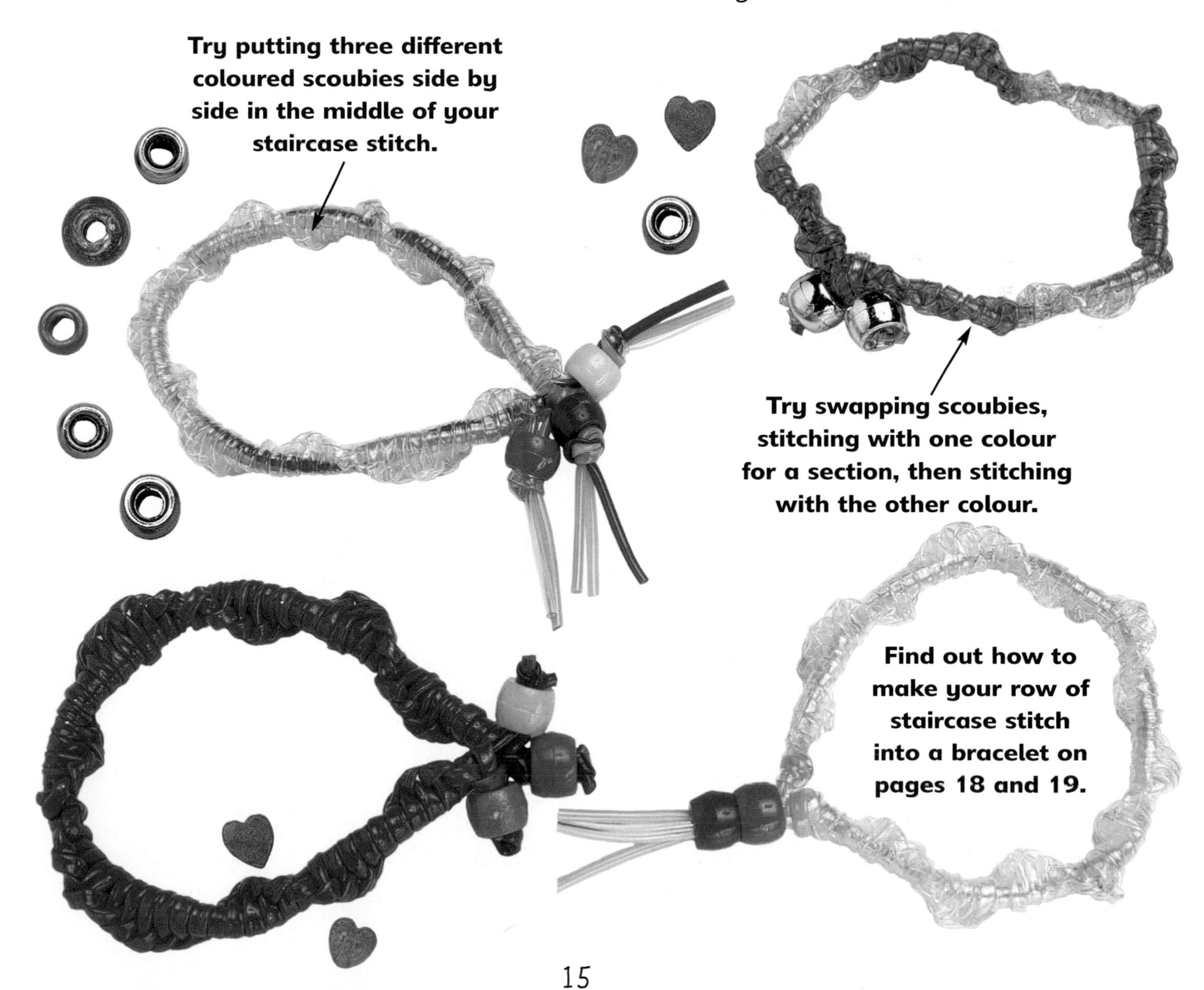

Colour Crazy

Make sure you use a scoubie in a colour that matches your mood. If you make a scoubie for a friend, choose a colour that sends a special friendship message. Check the list below for the traditional meanings behind scoubie colours.

Red
Your mood: "I'm in love."
Message to your friend: "I respect you."

White
Your mood: "I feel dreamy."
Message to your friend: "I think you're cool."

Yellow
Your mood: "I'm happy!"
Message to your friend: "You're a good mate."

Orange
Your mood: "I'm feeling positive."
Message to your friend: "You're amazing."

Pale pink
Your mood: "I'm chilled."
Message to your friend: "I admire you."

Deep pink
Your mood: "I'm excited!"
Message to your friend: "Thank you."

Black
Your mood: "Don't mess with me."
Message to your friend: "We're two of a kind."

Blue
Your mood: "I feel calm."
Message to your friend: "You can trust me."

Green
Your mood: "I feel thoughtful."
Message to your friend: "You're special."

Purple
Your mood: "I'm feeling sensitive."
Message to your friend: "Be my friend for ever."

A scoubie colour wheel

Choose scorchin' colour combos so your scoubies really rock.

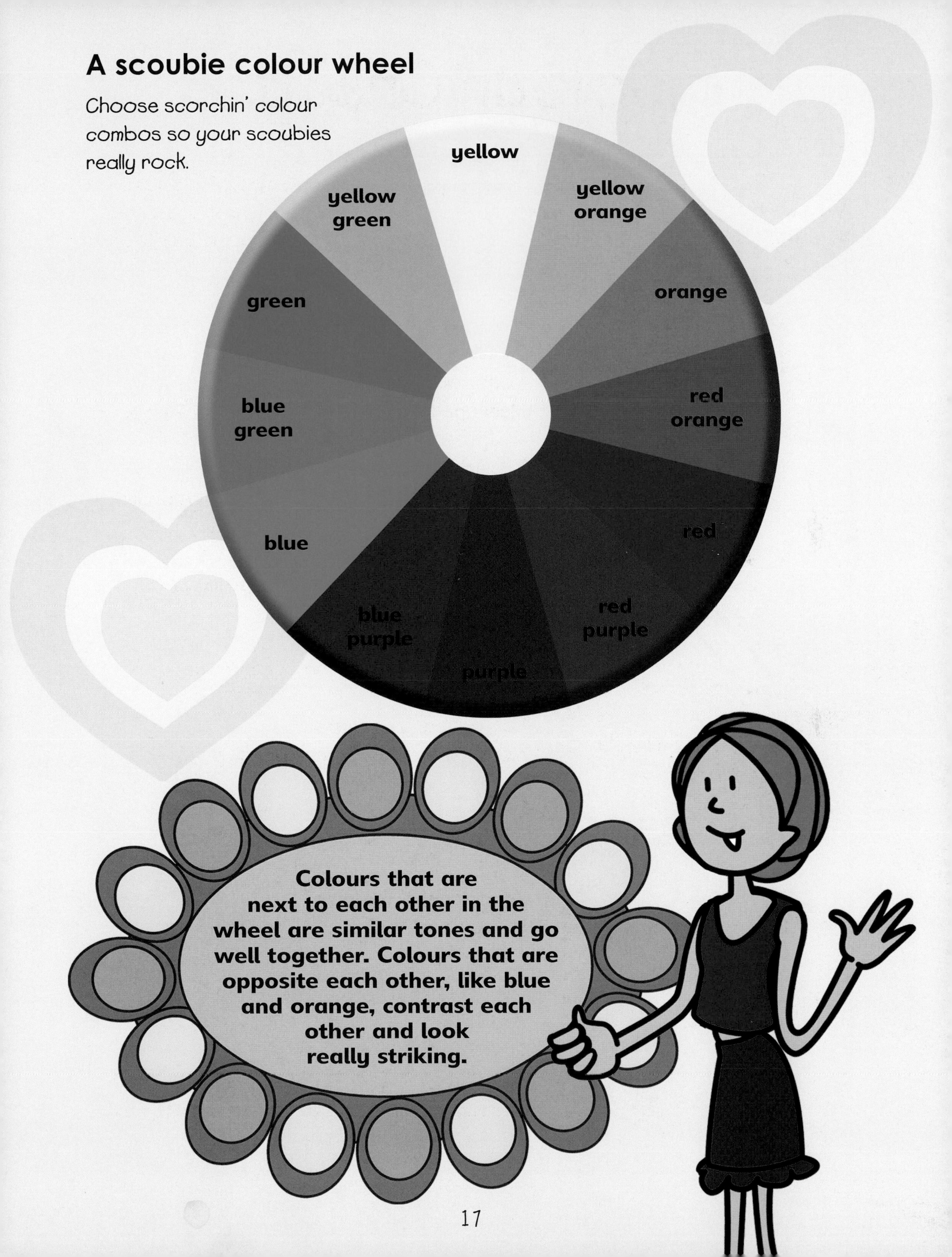

Finishing And Fixing

Are you wondering how to make a bracelet out of a row of scoubie stitching, and how to fix it on your wrist?

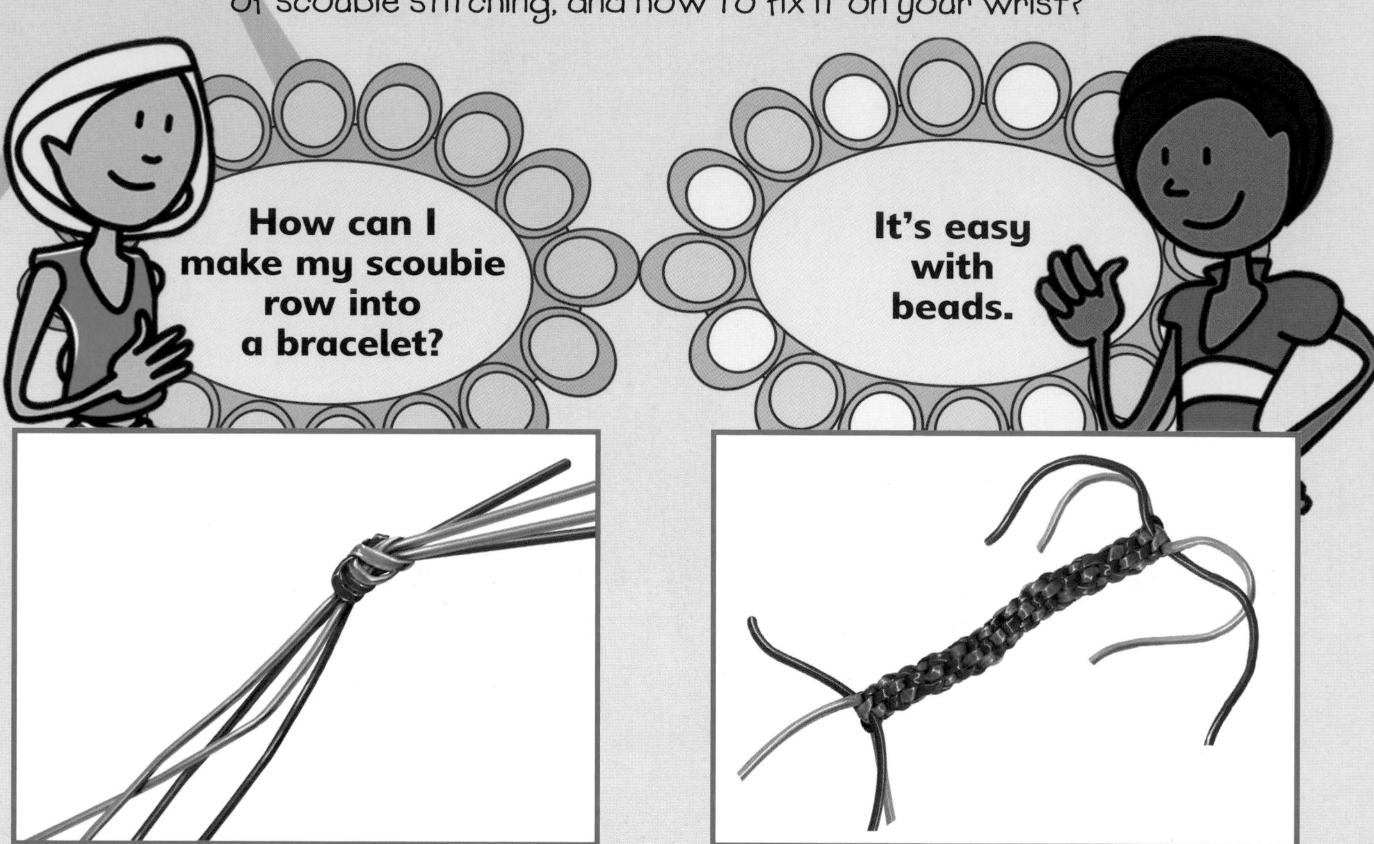

1. Tie four scoubies together with a loose knot as shown above. Leave about 3cm of scoubie above the knot.

2. At the end of your row leave 3cm of loose scoubie. Carefully untie the knot you made at the beginning.

3. Now pick a strand from each end of the row and thread both of them through a bead. Knot each one close to the bead.

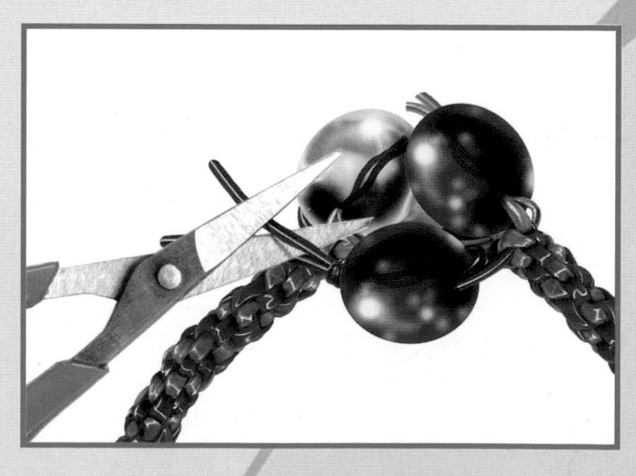

4. Repeat step **3** with other scoubie pairs, until all your loose scoubies are fixed through the beads. Then trim off the ends.

1. At the beginning of your row of stitching make a loop with one scoubie and tie the second strand around it.

2. At the end of your row of stitching, plait a 6cm length and add a bead before making a final knot.

3. Thread the plait through the loop and knot as above, or choose a large bead to squeeze through the loop.

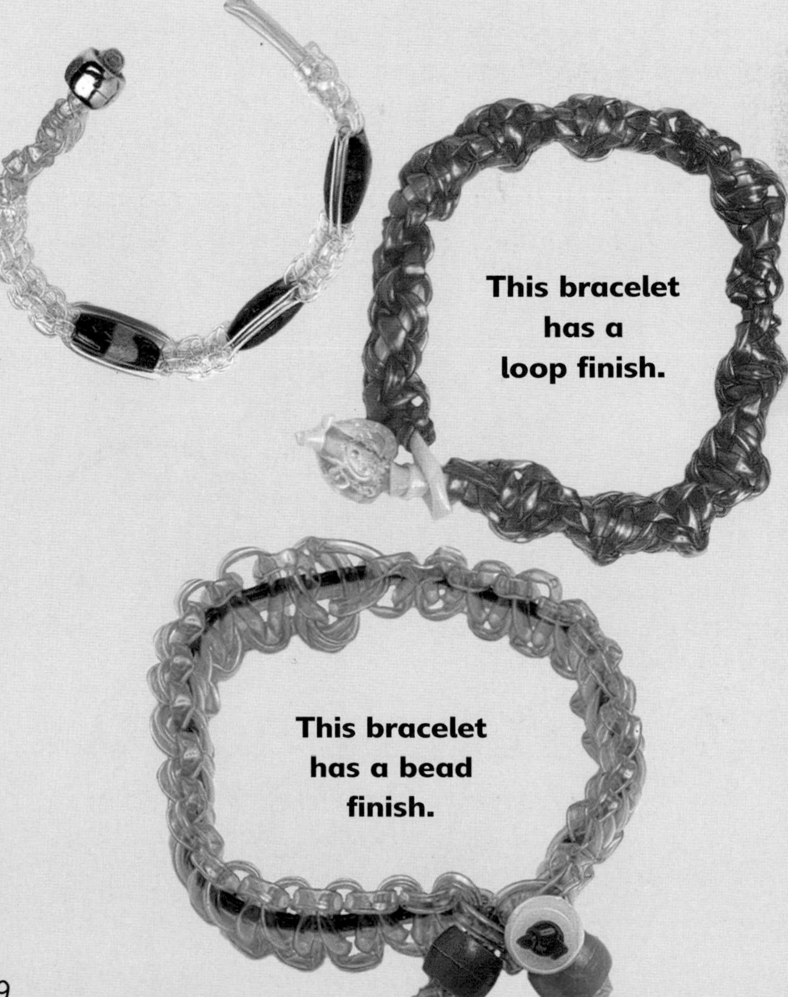

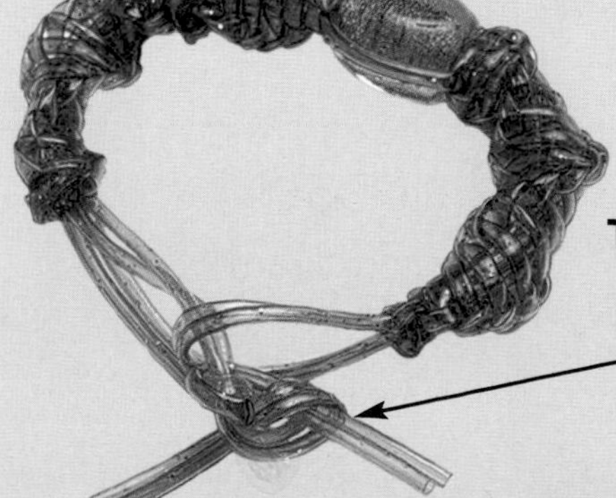

This bracelet is fastened with a loop and a simple knot.

Caterpillar Stitch

Caterpillar stitch is a totally spectacular scoubidou stitch! It will get you noticed, but the truly cool bit is that it is really easy to do. By the way, the caterpillar stitch gets its name because it lies flat, like a long fat caterpillar.

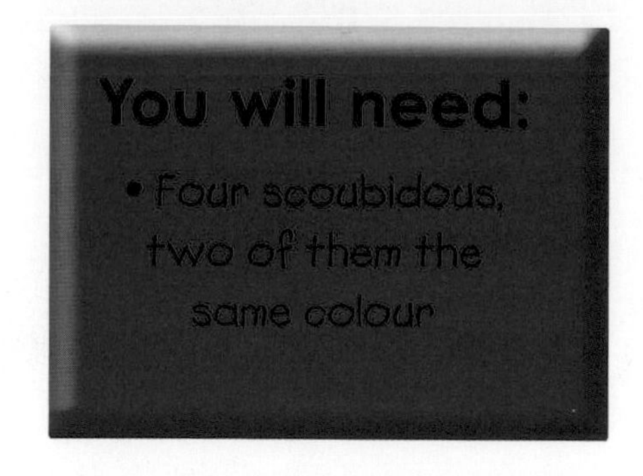

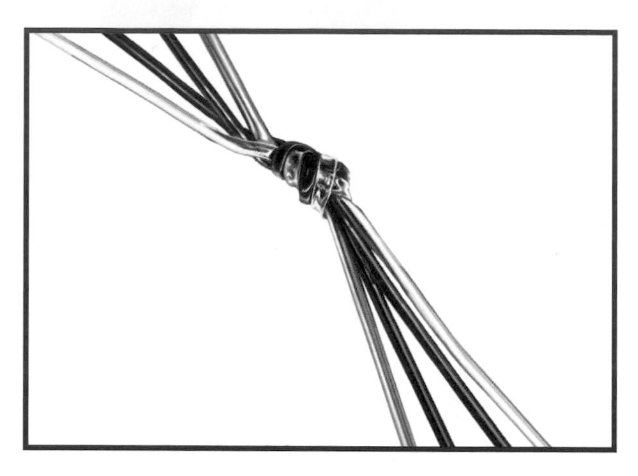

1. Tie the scoubidous together, leaving about 3cm of loose scoubidou above the knot. Pair up the two same-coloured ones in the middle.

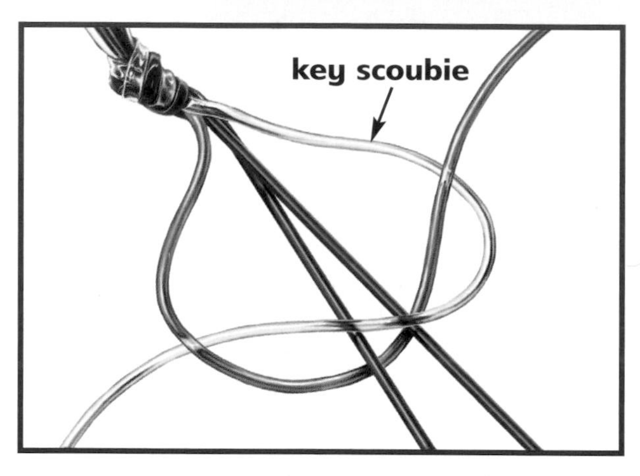

2. Start with the staircase stitch shown on page 14. Begin with the right-hand scoubie. This is your 'key' scoubie.

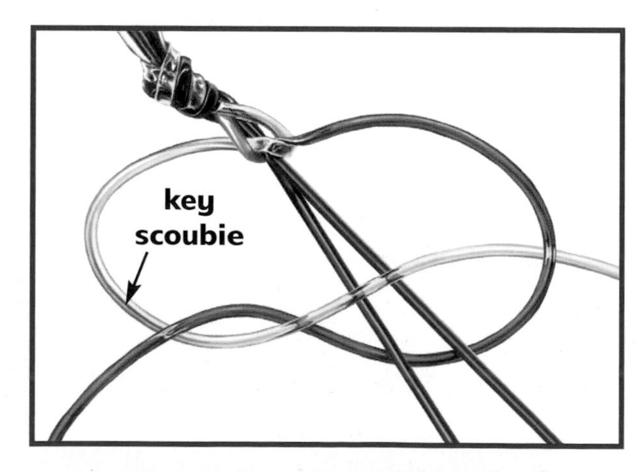

3. Do the same stitch the opposite way, starting with the key scoubie, which is now lying on the left-hand side.

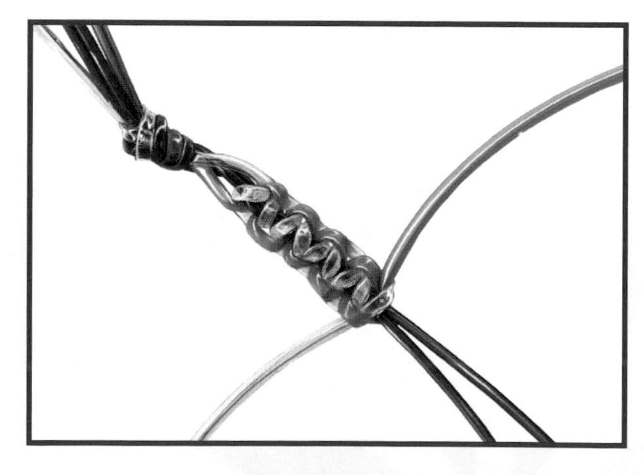

4. Keep doing the same stitch, starting from the right-hand side, then the left, then the right and so on. Always start with the key scoubie.

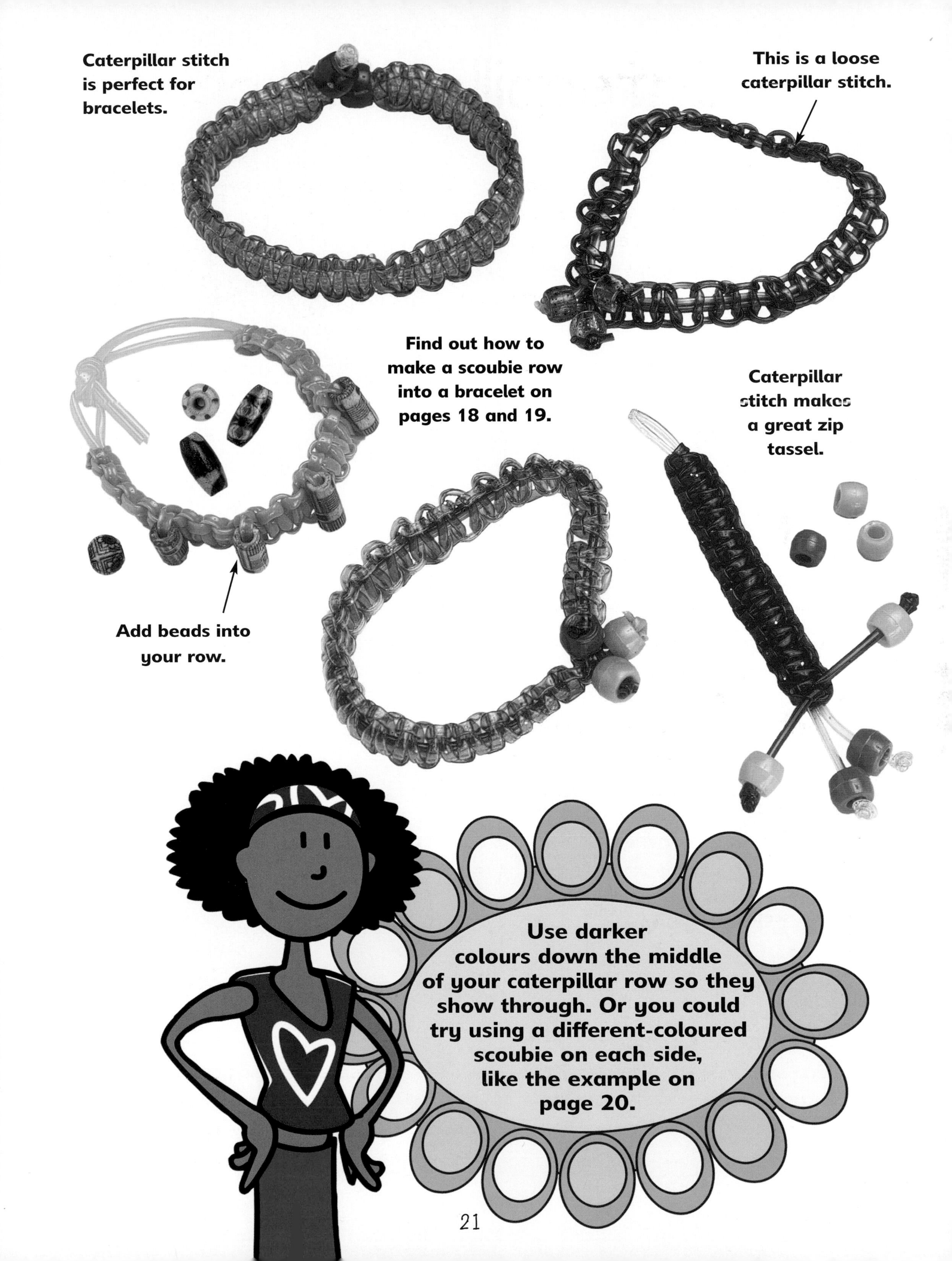
Caterpillar stitch
is perfect for
bracelets.
This is a loose
caterpillar stitch.
Find out how to
make a scoubie row
into a bracelet on
pages 18 and 19.
Caterpillar
stitch makes
a great zip
tassel.
Add beads into
your row.
Use darker
colours down the middle
of your caterpillar row so they
show through. Or you could
try using a different-coloured
scoubie on each side,
like the example on
page 20.

Surfin' Style

These surfin' wrist and ankle bracelets are simple, but ice cool. Wear them on hot sunny days, in a laid-back, surf-dude style.

You will need:

- A scoubidou (about 25cm long)
- Some seriously cool beads

Threading one big bead between two little ones looks good.

Metal beads will flash in the sunlight!

Customize your beads

Buy some plain wooden beads and paint them to make your own unique scoubidou jewellery. It's a good idea to push the beads on to an old knitting needle stuck into a lump of modelling clay. That way you can turn them easily to paint them and you won't paint your fingers! Once the paint is dry, coat the beads with PVA glue to make them shiny.

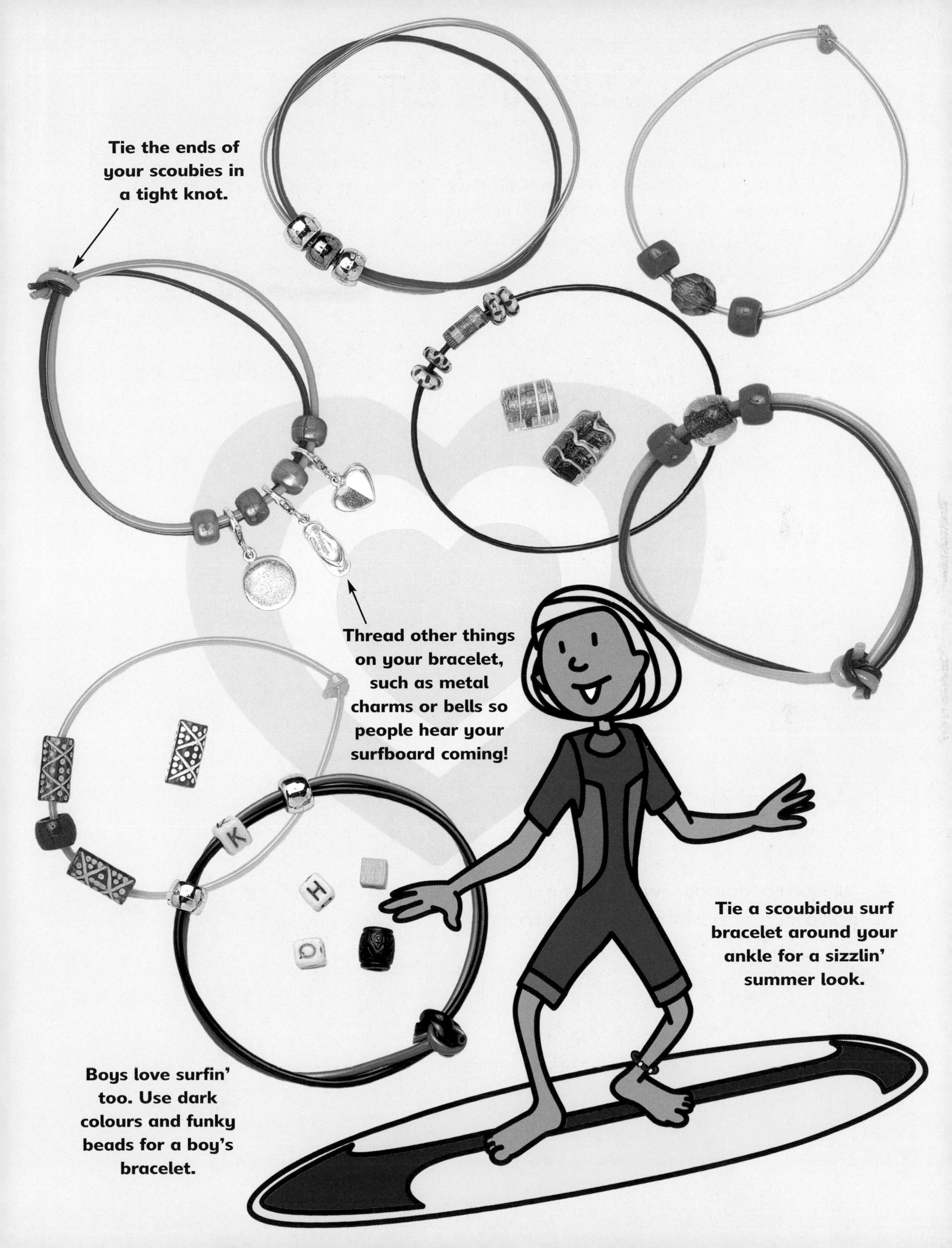
Tie the ends of your scoubies in a tight knot.
Thread other things on your bracelet, such as metal charms or bells so people hear your surfboard coming!
Tie a scoubidou surf bracelet around your ankle for a sizzlin' summer look.
Boys love surfin' too. Use dark colours and funky beads for a boy's bracelet.

Totally Wired!

All the best ears and wrists are wearing scoubidou earrings and bracelets. The ideal way to make them is using fine jewellery wire, because wire makes a scoubidou much easier to shape and work with. Plus your brilliant creations will last longer!

You will need:

- A scoubidou
- Fine jewellery wire
- A pair of earring wires
- Two amazing beads

Wire earrings

To make scoubie earrings with wire, thread the wire through a short scoubie strand. Leave a length of wire sticking out at the top and at the bottom.

At the top of your earring, use pliers to bend the end of the wire into a tiny loop. This loop will be used to fix your earring on to an earring wire (see page 56). You can buy packets of earring wires from craft shops.

You could wind the wired scoubie around a pencil to make it curl.

These earring wires are clip-ons.

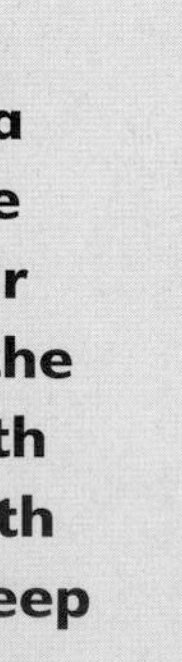

If you thread a bead on to the bottom of your earrings, bend the wire underneath the bead up with your pliers, to keep the bead in place.

Wire bracelets

Thread wire through a longer scoubie to make a bracelet. Decorate it with beads. Tie the ends of your bracelet together in a tight knot. Add a dot of PVA glue to the knot and trim the loose ends. If you can, hide the knot under a bead.

You will need:

- A scoubidou
- Fine jewellery wire
- A selection of beads

Rings And Things

Add some serious bling-bling to your fingers by making super scoubie rings with fabulous beads. For the best results, thread some fine jewellery wire through the middle of your scoubie first.

There are a couple of different ways to make scoubie rings and they are described below.

You will need:

- A short scoubidou that wraps around your finger with the ends overlapping slightly
- A beautiful bead
- Jewellery wire

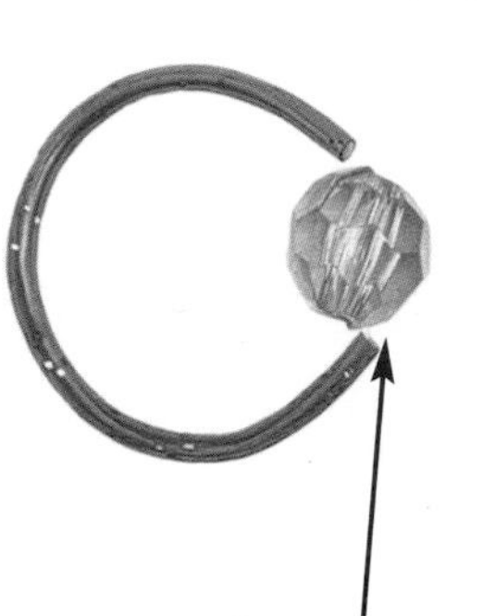

Put a drop of glue on each end of your scoubie and push them into the bead. Leave the glue to dry over night.

Thread the ends of the wire through the bead. Glue the ends of the scoubie to the sides of the bead.

Scoubie no-nos

We know that you're a sensible scoubidou-er, but just in case there are any scoubi-dunces out there, here's what NOT to do with a scoubidou:

- Let your pet eat one
- Let your little brother or sister chew one
- Tie one too tightly round your wrist or neck
- Melt one

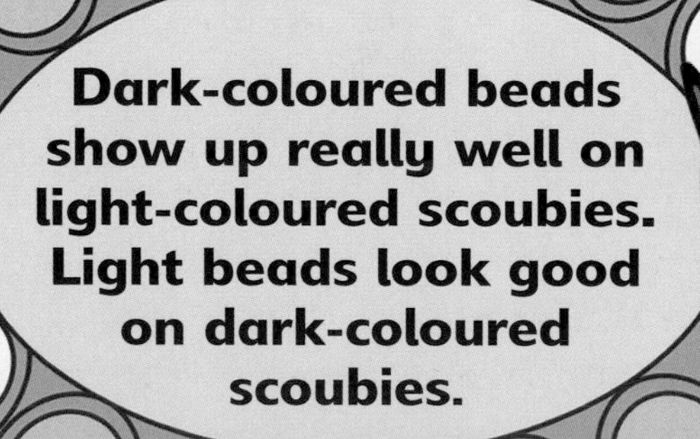

Dark-coloured beads show up really well on light-coloured scoubies. Light beads look good on dark-coloured scoubies.

Once you've successfully made a ring, try making a simple pair of loop earrings or the seriously cutting-edge loopy bracelet below.

How can I join the loop neatly?

To join two ends of a scoubie together neatly, cut one of the ends at an angle to make a point, dab on some glue and push it into the hole at the other end of the scoubie. Leave the glue to dry over night.

Thread the scoubidous through the loop on the earring wires.

Interlink scoubie loops until you have a bracelet of loops that fits around your wrist.

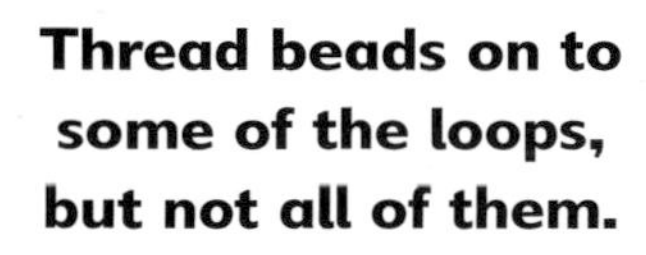

Thread beads on to some of the loops, but not all of them.

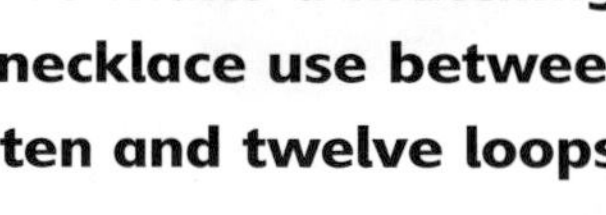

To make a matching necklace use between ten and twelve loops.

Scoubidou Birth Rings

Make a perfect personalized scoubie jewellery present for somebody's birthday by using beads that match the colour of their birthstones and scoubies that match their lucky colours.

The month you were born in determines which is your birthstone and which is your lucky colour. Here's the list of stones and lucky colours.

January
Lucky stone: Garnet (deep red)
Lucky colour: Turquoise

February
Lucky stone: Amethyst (pale purple)
Lucky colour: Silver

March
Lucky stone: Aquamarine (blue-green)
Lucky colour: Red

April
Lucky stone: Diamond (white)
Lucky colour: Brown

May
Lucky stone: Emerald (green)
Lucky colour: Orange

June
Lucky stone: Pearl (white)
Lucky colour: Yellow

July
Lucky stone: Ruby (red)
Lucky colour: Gold

August
Lucky stone: Peridot (green)
Lucky colour: Purple

September
Lucky stone: Sapphire (blue)
Lucky colour: Pink

October
Lucky stone: Opal (pink or blue)
Lucky colour: Blue

November
Lucky stone: Topaz (yellow)
Lucky colour: Black

December
Lucky stone: Turquoise (greenish-blue)
Lucky colour: Green

Groovy Scoubie Gift Ideas

You can make a gift for just about anyone with scoubies.
Here are some ideas but we are sure you will come up with lots more . . .

Make a cake with scoubie decorations on it.

Use wire to make a heart-shaped scoubie row for your Valentine.

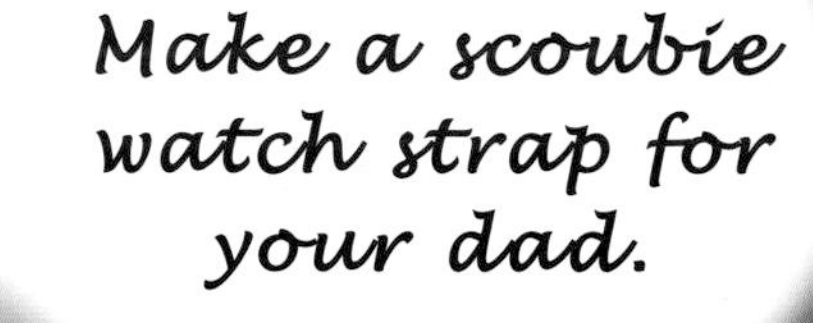

Make a scoubie watch strap for your dad.

Wrap scoubies around a plain belt for your sister.

Make a scoubie bookmark.

Decorate a card with loopy scoubies.

Use curly scoubies to tie up your gift parcels.

Wind scoubies around a hairband for a personal touch.

If your dad likes fishing, make him a "fly" out of colourful scoubies.

Glue a row of scoubie stitches around a photoframe.

Stitch a stormin' collar for your pet. Not too tight though!

Make your mum a glamorous set of jewellery with matching earrings, bracelet, necklace and a ring.

Bead It, Baby!

Once you've sussed out your favourite scoubidou stitch, get seriously sassy and bring beautiful beads into the mix.

You will need:

- Two scoubidous
- Billions of beads!

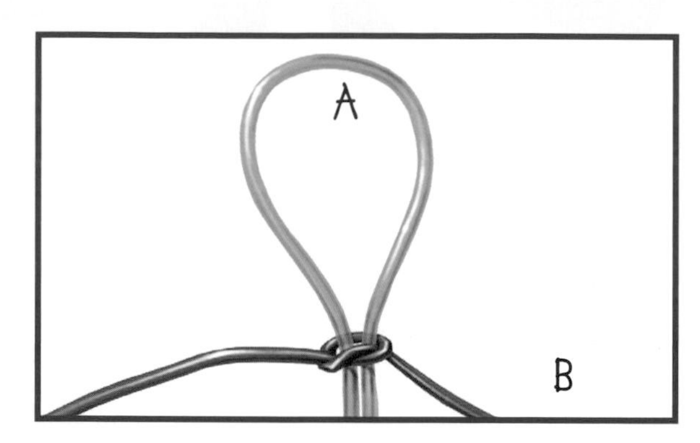

1. Fold scoubie A in half. Knot scoubie B near the top of A.

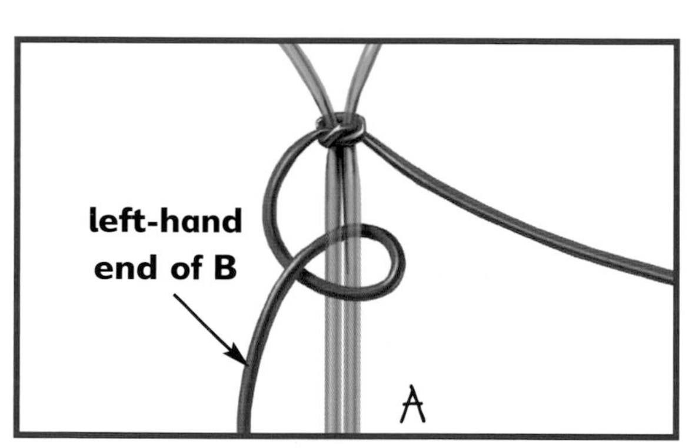

2. Loop the left-hand end of scoubie B around both strands of scoubie A.

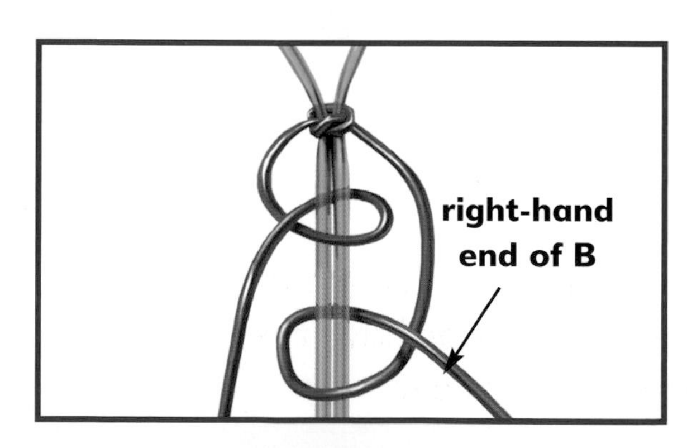

3. Now loop the right-hand end of scoubie B around scoubie A, and pull the stitches tight.

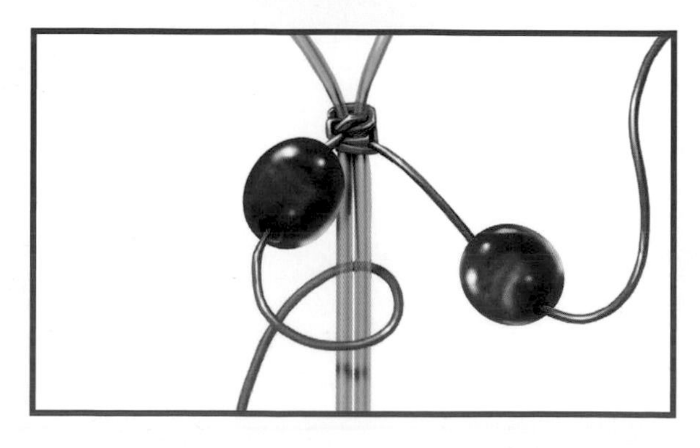

4. Thread a bead onto the left-hand end of B. Then repeat step **2**. Thread a bead on to the right-hand end of B and repeat step **3**. Keep repeating steps **2** to **4**.

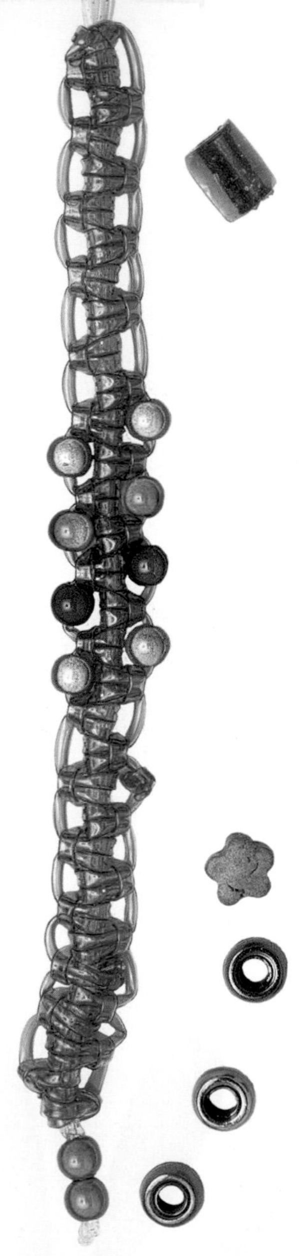

This is a truly funky way to add beads to your bracelet.

Loops and beads

Another way of adding beads is to create knotty loops and add a bead between each loop, as shown below.

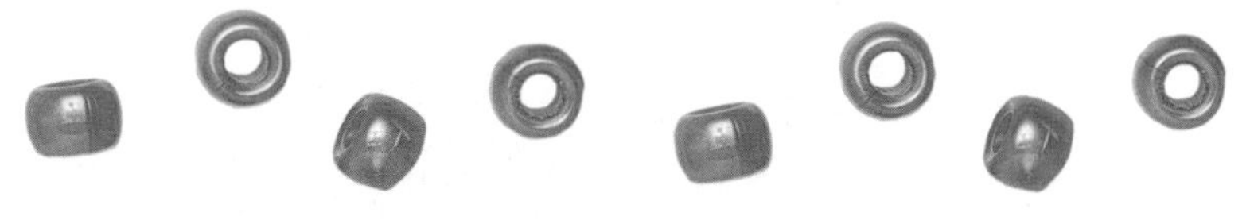

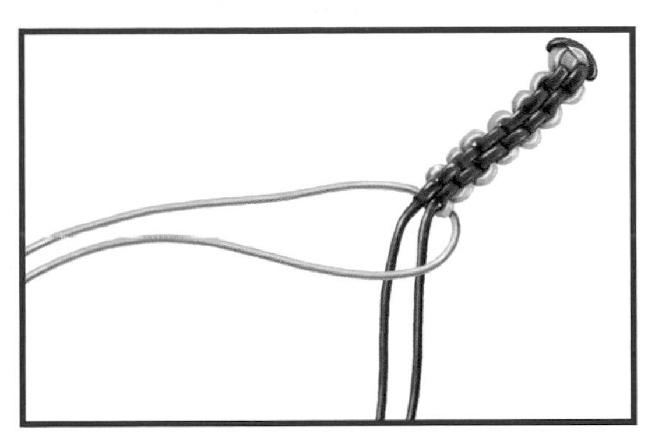

1. Begin with a starter knot (see page 6) and work a few square stitches (see page 8). Then separate out the scoubies into two pairs.

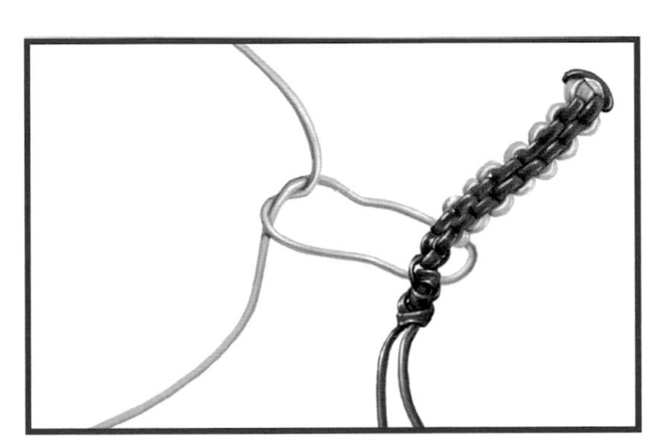

2. Tie simple knots along the length of each pair, as shown here. Knot alternate strands, but make sure you do the same number of knots on each side.

3. Push each pair through a bead (either through opposite ends of the bead as shown here, or through the same end). Repeat steps **2** and **3**, until you have the length you want.

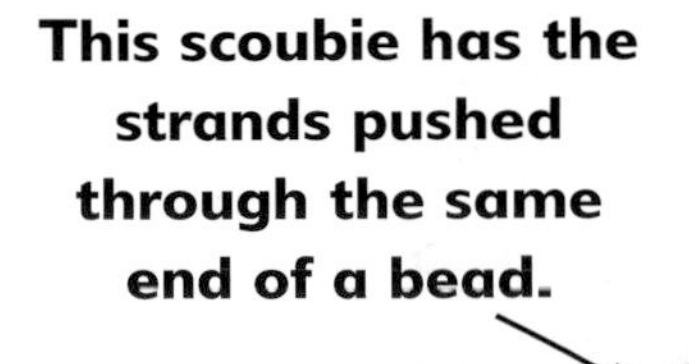

This scoubie has the strands pushed through the same end of a bead.

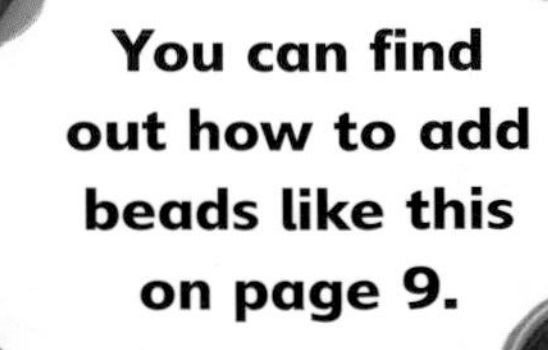

You can find out how to add beads like this on page 9.

What's Your Scoubie Style?

This quiz will reveal your true scoubie style. Pretend you're going shopping for clothes and choose your favourite item from each of these six lists.

1. TOP TOPS

a) A funky T-shirt
b) A sparkly party top
c) A floaty top, embroidered with flowers

2. LOVELY LEGS

a) Tracksuit pants in your favourite team's colours
b) Shorts with a sparkly belt
c) Embroidered jeans

3. FANCY DRESS PARTY

a) A Supergirl outfit
b) Cinderella's ballgown
c) A mermaid outfit

4. JEWELLERY

a) A bright plastic ring
b) A big African bangle
c) A gold necklace, discreet and delicate

5. COVER UP

a) A surf-label hoodie
b) A fun-fur coat
c) A brightly-coloured chunky jumper

6. TIME FOR BED

a) A T-shirt and shorts set
b) A pretty nightie
c) PJs with teddies on them

What do your answers mean?

OK, let's look in your shopping bag and sort out your fashion style!

Mostly a)s. Sporty Scoubie

You like practical, cool clothes that show everyone you're a sporty, all-action kind of girl. You'll suit the surf-dude scoubies on pages 22 and 23. Wear them when you go to collect your Olympic gold medal!

Mostly b)s. Party Scoubie

You're always up for a party because you love glamour. Try adding fabulous beads to your scoubies (see pages 32 and 33) and making dangly scoubie earrings (see page 24). Don't forget to wear them to your first Oscars ceremony!

Mostly c)s. Romantic Scoubie

You love floaty, flowery clothes and, in an ideal world, you'd be a Prom Queen! Choose pastel-coloured scoubies, such as pinks and purples. Hang beautiful plaited scoubies in your hair (see pages 36 and 37).

Party Plaits

Next time you want to create a stylin'-party look, wear plaited scoubies in your hair. Look out for sparkly or neon-coloured beads to add to your plait.

You will need:

- Three scoubidous
- Some beads

1. Fold the scoubies in half and use one of the strands to tie them together, so there is a 1.5cm loop at the top.

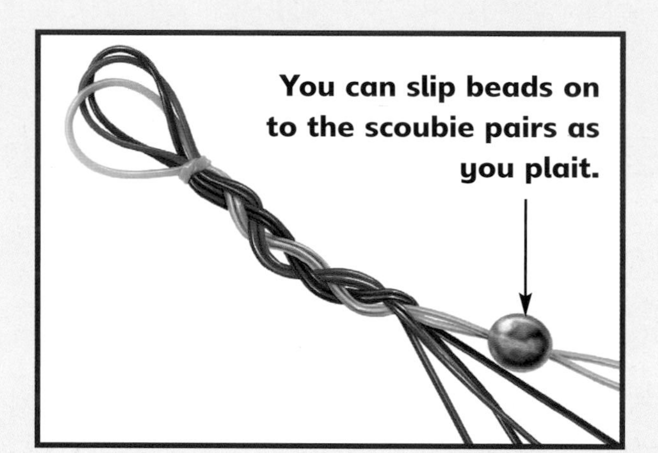

2. Separate the scoubies into three pairs and then plait the pairs together. Finish off with beads and knots.

Loosely knot the top of a scoubie to make a loop. Then knot beads along its length.

Thread a bunch of hair through the loop and pull it tight.

Glow-in-the-dark scoubies make fantastic jewellery to wear at Halloween.

Scoubie Pens

Have you seen how cool pens look when they've been scoubied? All you need is a pen or the tube from inside a ballpoint or gel pen. As you will see from the pictures on page 39, there are lots of ways to scoubie a pen, but here is an easy method.

You will need:

- Two or four scoubidous (the example below shows two scoubidous)
- A pen or pen inner inner

1. Tie the two scoubidous together at one end and do a starter knot (see page 6). Push the pen nib into the middle of the starter knot and pull the scoubies really tight.

2. Stitch around the pen inner – this picture shows square stitch, but circle stitch works well too. Pull the stitches tightly around the pen.

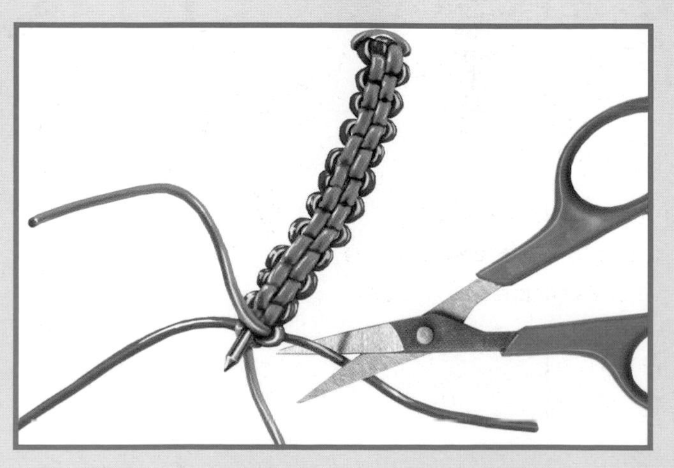

3. Make an extra stitch to cover the top of the pen. Then go back to the nib and untie the first big knot you made. Trim the loose scoubie ends at the top and bottom of the pen.

This pen uses both caterpillar and spiral stitch.
Slip a pompom on to the pen and knot your scoubies around it.
Add wires to your scoubies and curl the ends.
Decorate the top of the pen with beads.
To My Best Friend,
Scoubie House,
Scoubie Street,
Scoubieville
This pen is made by wrapping scoubies around the plastic case of a pen.

Cool Clips

You can stick a row of scoubie stitching on to a plain hair slide to create a fab and funky look. The example below shows a row of caterpillar stitch.

You will need:

- Three scoubidous for a single weave (as shown below) or five scoubies for a thicker double-weave
- A narrow hair clip or hair slide

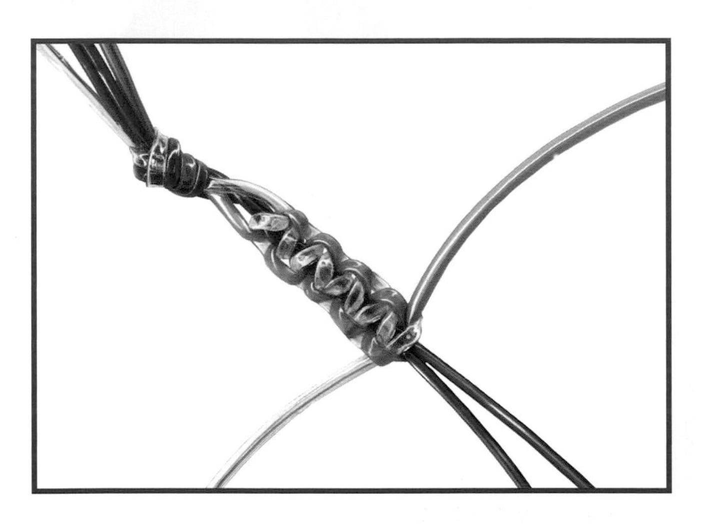

1. Follow the steps on page 20 to make a row of caterpillar stitch that is 1cm longer than your hair slide.

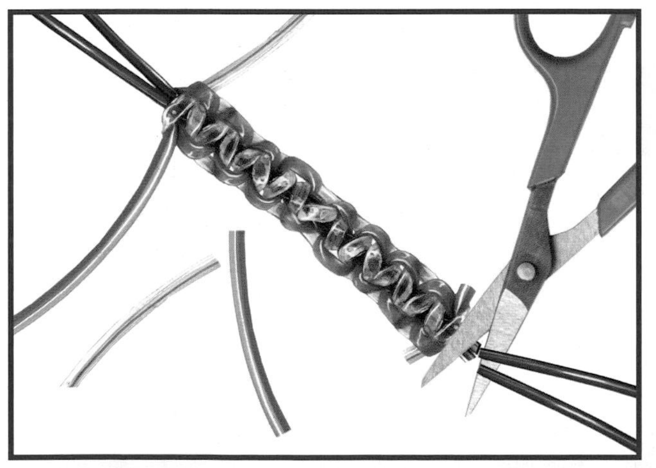

2. Tie the strands and pull them tight. Undo the first knot you made at the beginning and do the same thing.

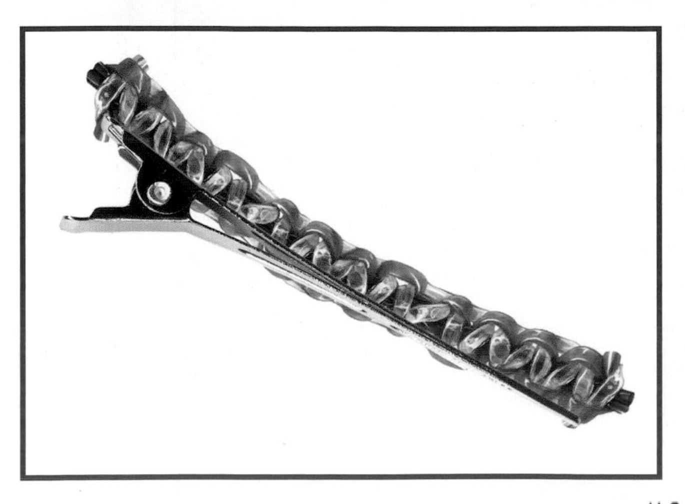

3. Trim the ends and dab glue at either end to keep everything in place, and leave to dry. When ready, glue your scoubie row on to the hair slide.

Stitch beads and bits of curly scoubie on to a hair slide to make a colourful piece of modern hair art. Here are some ideas to inspire you.

Go clip crazy and make a different design for every day of the week!

Form a scoubidou club with your mates, bring bags full of beads, pompoms, bells and feathers (and scoubies, of course) and swap them with your friends. Members could all have a matching bracelet to wear, in your club colours.

Freestyle!

Here's a selection of fun, funky and downright silly ways to use your scoubidous.

Set the world record for the longest plait.

Sell your scoubie creations at your school fair for charity.

Punch holes in your writing paper and weave scoubie strands through the holes.

Hang them off your lampshade – especially glow-in-the-dark ones. Don't let them melt!

Hang a scoubie from your mobile, so you always know which phone is yours!

Make scoubie decorations to hang on your Christmas tree.

Make mini-scoubies to hang from your school bag.

If you have a book of friendship-bracelet instructions, try some of the same stitches using scoubidous.

Mix up your stitches. What happens if you start with square stitch, swap to circle stitch or staircase stitch and back again?

Loop lots of brightly-coloured scoubidous around your bedposts.

Use scoubies as shoelaces to funk up your trainers.

Build an incredibly complicated scoubie sculpture and win an art prize.

Get your friends stitching and make a rainbow-coloured skipping rope.

Tie scoubies to the sides of your sunnies.

Use scoubies to take over the universe.

Loopy Scoubies

Here are some really cool necklaces
for special occasions.
All you have to do is go loopy!

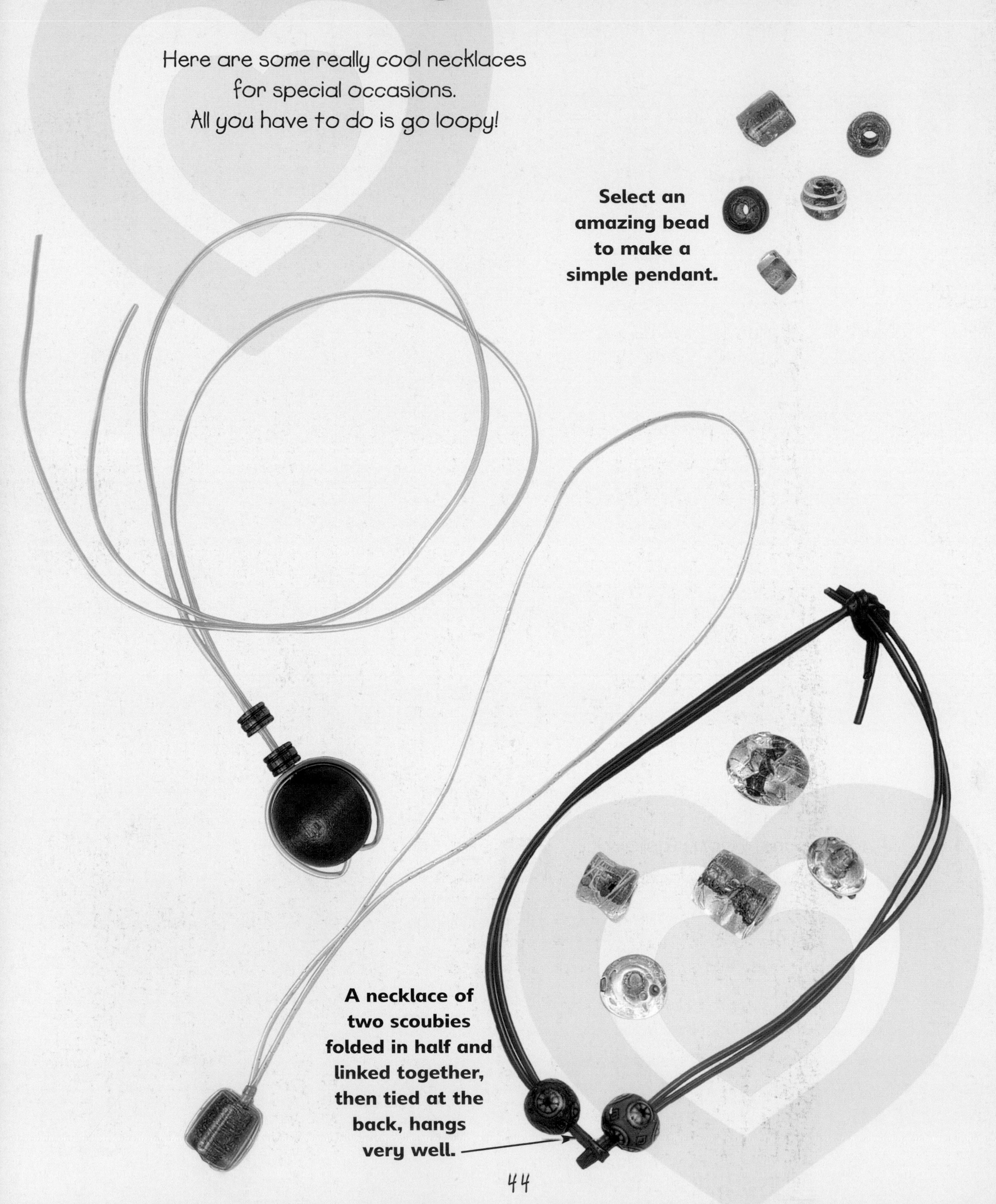

Select an amazing bead to make a simple pendant.

A necklace of two scoubies folded in half and linked together, then tied at the back, hangs very well.

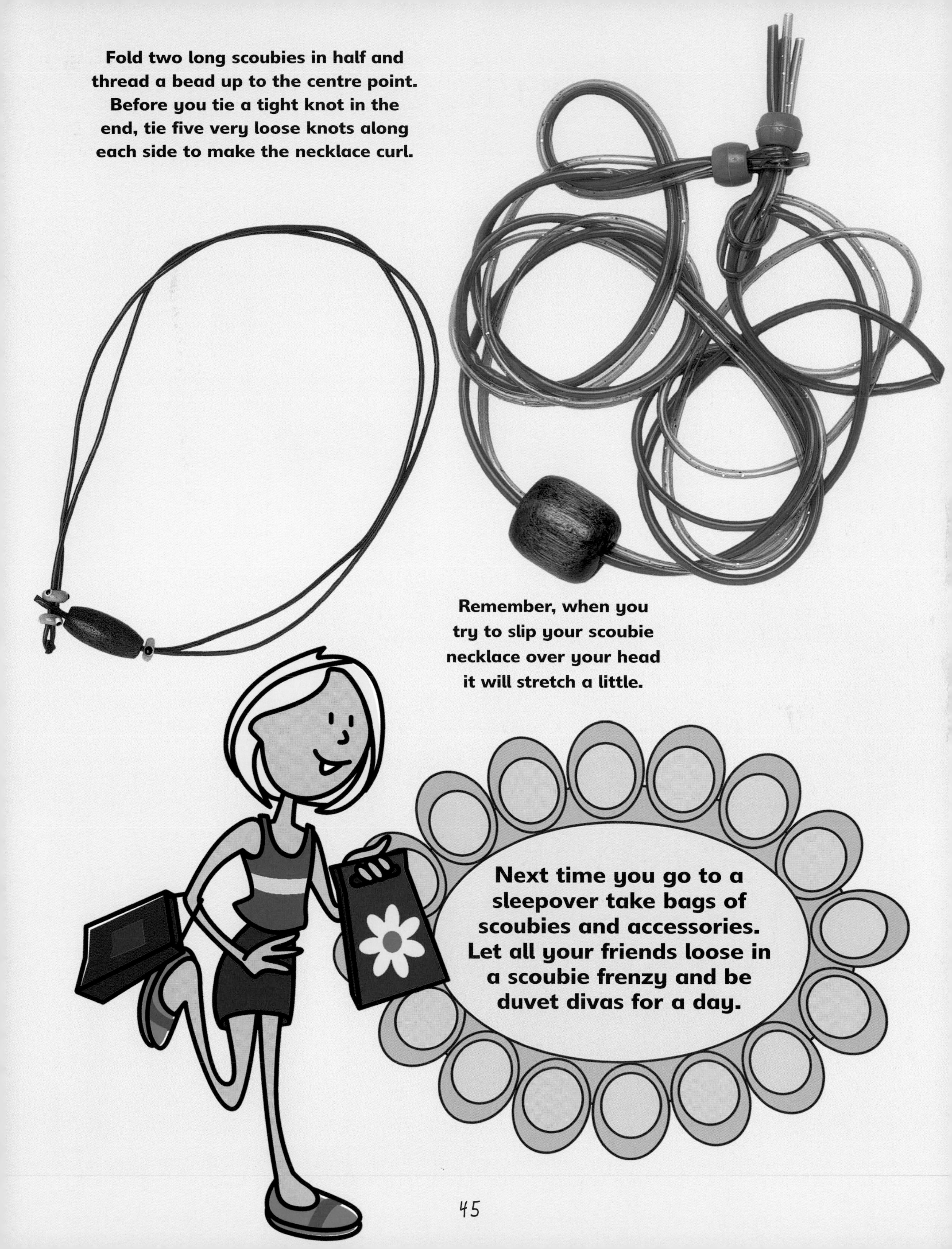

Fold two long scoubies in half and thread a bead up to the centre point. Before you tie a tight knot in the end, tie five very loose knots along each side to make the necklace curl.

Remember, when you try to slip your scoubie necklace over your head it will stretch a little.

Next time you go to a sleepover take bags of scoubies and accessories. Let all your friends loose in a scoubie frenzy and be duvet divas for a day.

Worldwide Scoubies

Here are some scorchin' colour palettes showing mixtures of different colours which are typically used in places around the world. They will give you some international inspiration for your scoubies.

Arabian Lands – use red, orange, yellow and blue.

African Adventure – use brown, red, yellow and white.

French, British or American Dream – use red, white and blue.

Indian Intrigue – use turquoise, yellow, purple and green.

Jamaican Joy – use green, yellow and black.

Mediterranean Marvel – use dark blue, light blue and white.

Ollie 'n' Olga

These gorgeous little critters are called Ollie and Olga. They are probably the easiest scoubidou creatures to make.

We think everybody should have an Ollie or an Olga. Here's how to make Ollie.

You will need:

- Four scoubidous
- A pair of eyes (from a craft shop)
- A split ring, to make Ollie into a keyring
- Eight beads

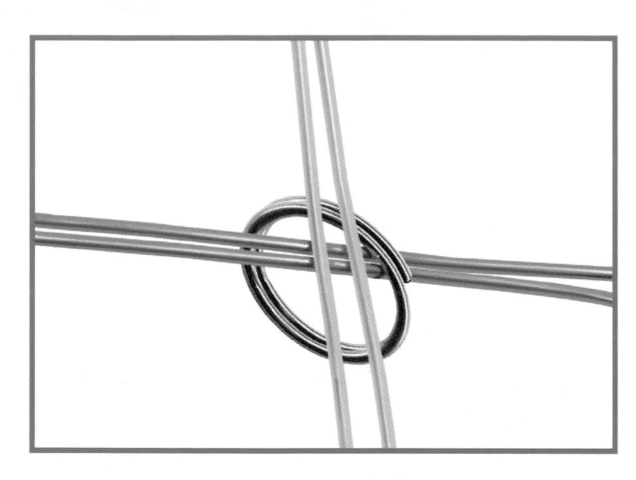

1. Split the scoubies into two pairs. Place the middle of one pair through the split ring. Place the other pair on top of the ring to form a cross.

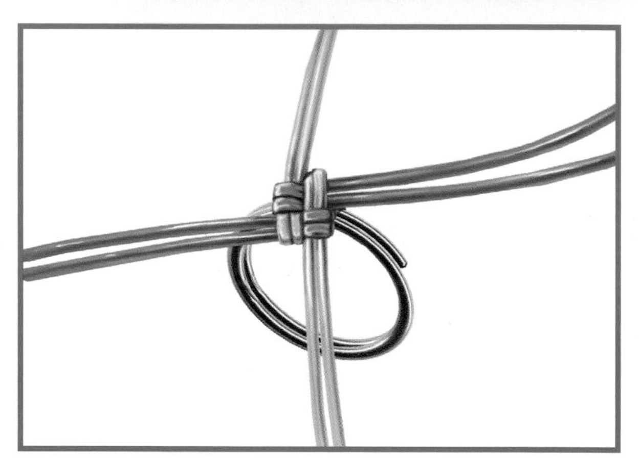

2. Do a starter knot (see page 6) followed by some square stitches (see page 8) for about 3cm. The threads left loose at the bottom should be 5cm or longer.

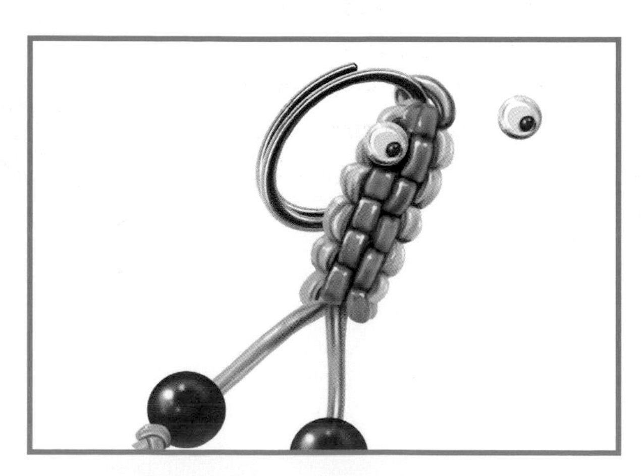

3. Snip off four of the loose ends to leave Ollie two legs. Tie on two beads and stick on some eyes.

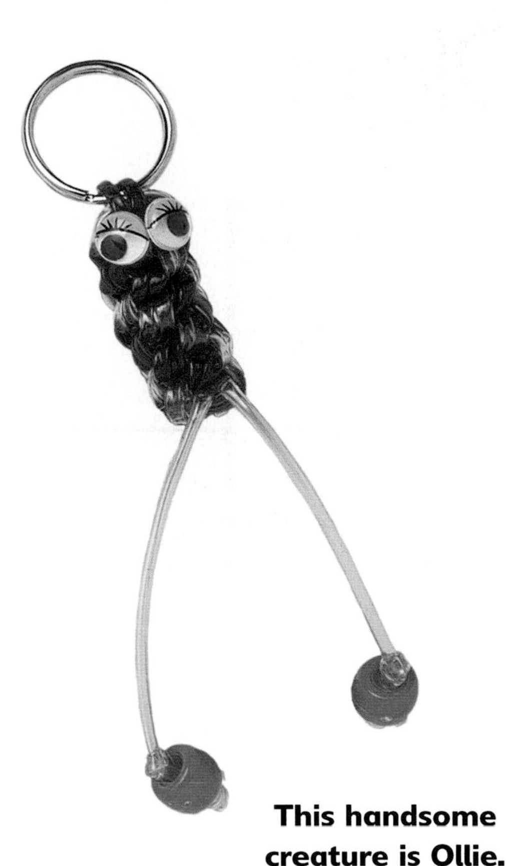

This handsome creature is Ollie.

If you like Ollie and Olga

- Make a whole family of Ollies and Olgas. Line them up on your windowsill or on top of your computer.
- Hang Ollie on a necklace or make two tiny Ollies into fun earrings.
- Hang an Olga in your mum's car.
- Attach an Ollie to a birthday card for your best friend and write "With love from me and Ollie".
- See how big you can make an Ollie, and how small!
- Hang several Ollies and Olgas on scoubidous of different lengths, then tie them to a coathanger to make a mobile.

To make Olga, slip a bead onto the two scoubies before you start stitching and use staircase stitch (see page 14).

Scoubie Wordsearch

Can you find the scoubie words hidden in the grid below?
(You will find the answers on page 55.)

SCOUBIDOUS
KEYRINGS
BRACELET
EARRINGS
NECKLACE
SQUARE STITCH
CATERPILLAR
CIRCLE STITCH
STAIRCASE
FUNKY

S	O	E	S	A	C	R	I	A	T	S	Q	F	B	C
C	I	R	C	L	E	S	T	I	T	C	H	M	A	I
U	F	A	I	F	M	R	C	A	U	J	E	T	R	P
B	A	G	C	R	Y	E	B	R	A	C	E	L	E	T
K	N	E	V	N	I	C	A	S	N	R	Q	K	C	D
E	C	A	L	K	C	E	N	T	P	V	F	S	O	E
F	T	L	X	S	E	V	T	I	L	P	U	M	B	A
L	D	I	C	Q	T	Y	L	A	K	O	J	E	T	R
W	S	Y	A	U	C	L	R	R	D	S	W	S	B	R
G	C	K	M	E	A	S	P	I	Y	V	M	F	Y	I
H	A	N	B	R	H	T	B	C	N	A	E	L	H	N
A	L	U	O	S	C	U	L	A	O	G	P	H	Z	G
V	E	F	D	T	O	I	L	S	U	L	S	V	F	S
E	F	S	E	C	I	T	B	F	T	M	B	N	M	G
N	R	T	S	Q	U	A	R	E	S	T	I	T	C	H